BE A WINE AND BEER JUDGE

Be a Wine and Beer Judge

—a guide for the lover of
wines and beers, both amateur
and commercial

FIRST EDITION

First Impression   February 1977

---

by

S. W. ANDREWS

Chairman, A. W. National Guild of Judges

Amateur Winemaking Publications Ltd.
Andover, Hants.

ISBN 0 900841 47 8

Printed in Great Britain by:

Standard Press (Andover) Ltd., South Street, Andover, Hants.

Contents

Cover and Photographs by: Charles Torrington
High Barnet, Hertfordshire.

Beer Judging Chapters by: Wilf Newsom

Line diagrams by: Rex Royle

Introduction

The Amateur Winemaking movement in this country continues to grow, and with it the desire of a great number of its members to learn more about the assessment of quality and faults of wine.

This book has been written to provide the aspirant judge of amateur wine with detailed information how the senses are used in the assessment of wine and beer, also to give more general information to those who are actively engaged in organising, stewarding and judging at Wine and Beer Shows.

It is hoped that this book will stimulate interest in the subject, and so lead to new enthusiasts taking up the art, or science of wine tasting and judging.

Wine tasting is a very complex exercise, many people drink wine without ever really tasting it; this is a great pity as wine has so much to offer. To savour the bouquet, flavour and aroma of a good wine is a gustatory experience without equal. It is not an experience to be hurried, wine should be savoured leisurely, and enjoyed to the full.

Man's awareness is limited to the extent of his reaction to a special nerve stimulus. Many happenings pass unnoticed, either because they are below the threshold of man's perception, and so do not arouse a reaction, or because man does not possess the necessary nerve organs to respond to a certain stimulus.

The assessment of wine involves the use of all of our special senses, i.e. sight, smell, taste, touch and to a small extent—hearing.

Memory also plays a very important part in assessing wines, as only by remembering certain smells or tastes can we make comparisons.

Every person has a sense of smell and of taste. However, the efficiency of the senses varies a great deal between individuals. If one has a palate it is possible to train and develop it until it reaches a high degree of efficiency. If on the other hand, the palate is ignored, and no effort is made to improve it, its efficiency will remain at a low level.

The unfortunate section of the populace who have no natural palate will of course not be able to give a critical assessment of wine. This will not prevent them from enjoying their wine and having a very definite opinion of it. At the same time they will not be able to appreciate the finer taste points, or the quality of wine.

Work in this field (Fisher and Griffin 1961) shows that because of differences in the enzyme systems of their saliva, approximately 30 per cent of the white population show anomalies in their taste thresholds.

As the special senses play such an important part in wine assessment, it is advisable to understand a little of the way in which they work.

It is then possible to appreciate how their efficiency can be affected by outside influences. A lowered body temperature, pain, a light infection of the ear, anger, fatigue, either mental or physical, or sadness can all affect ones critical perception. These physiological and psychological factors may not be taken into account by many wine tasters, yet they can have a marked effect on the efficiency of their tasting. In the following chapters I shall be dealing very briefly with the physiology of the senses; this will enable the reader to understand how apparently unconnected factors can have important bearings on the evaluation of wine.

For the Chapter on beer Judging I am greatly indebted to my old friend, Wilf Newsom, the original Beer Judge of them all!

Chapter 1

On becoming a judge

Most of us—and by "us" I mean winemakers—rather fancy ourselves as judges of wine, and it is certainly true that most of us "know what we like". That is a far cry, however, from being a *judge* of wine, from being able to assess a large number of wines against one another, placing the best of them in order of merit, and then being able to give exhibitors logical and acceptable reasons for one's decisions.

Many enthusiastic winemakers would dearly like to be able to do this, and to become accepted by their fellow-hobbyists as sound and reliable judges, looked up to and respected for their knowledge and wine appreciation, but they are not quite sure how to set about gaining the necessary technique and experience. Many are content to judge within the confines of their own wine circle competitions, but others aspire to become judges at large Federation shows—competitions held by groups of clubs in particular areas—or even at national level. Many, too, keenly desire to become members of the Amateur Winemakers National Guild of Judges, a highly respected body of wine judges whose badge is coveted and proudly worn. It is to help all these would-be judges, and to amplify the essential but rather bald instructions to be found in the Guild's little handbook on the subject that I have written this more detailed book.

"I wish to become a National Judge" are words that I have often heard from amateur winemakers, and it is one that I am delighted to hear, but I do sometimes wonder if its implications are fully understood.

There is no quick or easy way to become a National judge of wine or beer. It is greatly enjoyable, of course, to the wine lover, but is not a task to be undertaken lightly, or by those only weakly motivated. It demands years of application, learning the theory of winemaking, putting that theory into practice by making all types of wine, thereby gathering knowledge from both successes and failures. Also, by preparing and entering wine in competitive exhibition you will reach a standard of perfection that will enable you to win top awards at the larger wine shows. In this way, you will prove your ability to not only make quality wines but, equally important, to recognise good wines when selecting your entries.

Obviously, any would-be judge must have a good palate for wine and be able to detect and identify the various components of it, appreciate wine quality and, mainly through practical experience in winemaking, have a good basic knowledge of wine imperfections, their cause and origin, how to prevent them and, where applicable, their cure. This you will acquire by tasting, re-tasting, examining and analysing wine at every available opportunity and, most important, making a conscious effort to remember the subjective impressions gained during these experiences. Volunteer to steward for a National

Judge at every available opportunity, observe the judge's procedure, and remember all that he tells you during the judging session. Quite a formidable programme, you may think, but you will find the task both stimulating and rewarding, and you will at all times receive help and encouragement from members of The Amateur Winemakers National Guild of Judges, whose role is explained in Chapter 13.

Chapter 2
Training your palate

It goes without saying that any judge of wine, who needs to make fine distinctions of smell and taste, must have a highly developed palate. Every normal person has the senses of smell and taste, but that is not to say that they have a palate which is equipped with the physical and sensory requirements of a wine judge. Some people, through no fault of their own, are unable to appreciate wine, because of deficiencies in their palate structure, deficiencies which may be inherited or caused by illness or injury. To this unfortunate section of the community, no amount of training will bring any improvement, so the first step is to ascertain whether in fact you have a palate. There is a very simple test for recognition of the four basic tastes involved, i.e. sweetness, sourness (acidity), saltiness and bitterness, but unless you are conversant with the preparation of small amounts of chemical substances in solution, it is better to seek the assistance of a chemist friend. Your local chemist will probably make for you the required test solutions.

You need solutions in water containing sugar, acid, salt and quinine.

Solution A.   1.6 per cent solution of sugar in water
Solution B.   0.3 per cent solution salt in water
Solution C.   0.1 per cent solution citric acid in water
Solution D. 0.001 per cent solution quinine sulphate in water

For the test, mark four identical glasses A, B, C and D. This can be done by affixing a small label on the base of the glass so that it cannot be read accidentally. Pour a sample of each solution into its correct glass, then seek the help of another person. Ask your helper to rearrange the glasses without your knowing the order—you can leave the room whilst this is being done. Then come back in and taste each solution in turn, "blind", rinsing your mouth with water between each tasting. Rinsing your mouth is not essential but it is as well to establish this practice at once. Make a note of what you can taste and at the end, compare your result with the order given. A person with a normal palate should be able to detect the different tastes using solutions of the above concentrations. Should the first test prove inconclusive, do not be discouraged but repeat the test until you *are* able to identify them. You may, of course, be amongst the unfortunate section of people who are unable to recognise these tastes but if you are a successful competitor there is little doubt that you also have a palate.

Having recognised the solutions, you may now proceed to experiment further by diluting the solutions with 25 per cent water and repeating the test, repeating the dilutions until you can no longer separate the tastes. This exercise will indicate your threshold level for the various substances. As the recognition of saltiness has little value in wine tasting, we are left with sweetness, acidity and bitterness.

A more simple way of testing your palate reaction to varying amounts of acid and sugar in solution, and one which requires hardly any preparation, is as follows:

You will require: Citric acid

Heavy sugar syrup

Four identical glasses

A Pipette

Acid Test—Dissolve one level teaspoonful of citric acid in two teaspoons of water. Mark your glasses A, B, C and D. Pour 15 mls. (approximately half an ounce) of water into each glass. Then, using the pipette, add four drops of citric acid solution to glass A, eight to glass B, and 12 to glass C. No addition is made to glass D. Now ask your helper to rearrange the glasses, then taste your samples. Mark your results in the order in which you taste them, i.e. neutral, low, medium or high acid. Repeat if necessary. There may be a little confusion at first between B and C. Having placed them correctly, taste them again and concentrate on your memory impressions of each sample.

Sugar Test—Now repeat the experiment for sugar recognition. Using heavy sugar syrup, made by dissolving $\frac{1}{2}$ lb. sugar in five ounces of water, you can make up a smaller amount, but use the same ratio of sugar to water. Using the same amount of water as for the acid test, add six drops of syrup to glass A, 12 to glass B, and 18 to glass C. No addition is made to glass D. Stir the samples, and repeat the process of rearranging the sample glasses. Mark your result in the order in which you taste the samples either neutral, low, medium or high sugar. Having assessed them correctly, taste again. Concentrate on their impressions on your palate and memorise them. Having established your palate recognition for various levels of acid and sugar solutions, now experiment with a mixture of the two.

Prepare your glasses as before, but this time use all the glasses for the combination of solutions. Into glass A add six drops of syrup and four of acid, into glass B add 12 of syrup and eight of acid, into glass C add 18 drops of syrup and 12 of acid, into glass D add 24 drops of syrup and 14 of acid. Proceed as for the previous experiments. The low acid samples will provide no difficulty but there may be some confusion between the higher acid samples at first.

You will probably find this experiment at first a little confusing, for the sugar will soften the tartness of the acid. Nevertheless, with perseverance you should be able to distinguish between the samples. You will probably have to taste the samples several times before arriving at a decision. This test will give you a good idea of how the acid and sweet tastes are recognised and separated by the palate; concentrate first on the sweetness and then on the acidity. As you proceed with your palate training, you may wish to experiment further by varying the amounts of sugar and acid additions, such as, adding low acid to high sugar, medium acid to low sugar etc. You will find that four drops of acid to 24 of sugar will provide a plesant combination and that you will be able to taste the acid quite clearly, but add six drops of sugar to 14 of acid and the sweet taste will be difficult to distinguish. By increasing the ratio of 12 drops of sugar syrup to 14 of acid you will again recognise the sweet taste, although the solution will taste quite acid.

Recognition of the basic components of wine is

more complex because each component exerts an influence on its fellow. This is particularly true of alcohol, but there are one or two basic tests that you can carry out.

For the first, use a lightly-flavoured wine such as dry gooseberry or apple. Make up three small bottles of this wine and ask a friend who has a good palate to increase the acidity in one sample until it is easily recognisable by comparison with the other two samples, then code the bottles. Do the same with an identical red wine that has a low tannin content and ask him to increase the tannin content in one of the samples, again coding the bottles. You then sample each set of wines and find the odd one out.

Another test is to find out whether you can tell the difference between acidity and astringency, because there is some confusion by some winemakers between these two. For this test you will require four bottles of identical red wine. This time, acid is added to one sample and tannin to another, the remaining two samples have no addition and the bottles should again be carefully coded. In this test, you have to find the over-acid and the over-astringent wines. A similar test can be prepared by adding sugar syrup to one of the test samples. Another slightly more complicated test can be prepared by using six small bottles of identical red wine, adding acid to one, tannin to another, and acid and tannin to a third, leaving three bottles without additions. Again, careful coding is necessary and the taster should find and identify the three additions. These tests can also be used in Winemaking Circles as part of a palate appreciation evening.

Having established that you have a palate is but the

first step on the road to becoming a judge. Your palate will need training to increase its efficiency. Training the palate is done in two phases, one you can do yourself and the other requires the help of another person knowledgeable in wine tasting and who has a good palate.

There are many things you can do yourself. Firstly, and this is a most enjoyable exercise, drink and analyse as many wines as you like—your own, those of your friends, both home-made and commercial ones of all types and varieties.

The training of the palate must be a conscious effort. In the beginning, it is advisable to concentrate on one aspect only. First of all, concentrate on the **smell** of the wine, analyse it and remember the impressions it gave you. When tasting wine, concentrate first of all on the **sweetness**, then the **acidity,** next the **astringency,** then the **alcohol** content, the **flavour,** the body or "feel" of the wine in the mouth and lastly, the **overall impression.** You should do this every time you are offered a glass of wine—for the first two mouthfulls, then drink the remainder at leisure and enjoy it! You will find that after a time you are doing this from habit; you may even find yourself subconsciously sniffing a cup of tea!

Take every opportunity to attend wine tastings, both of home-made and commercial wines. Go with the express purpose of increasing your palate appreciation and knowledge of wine, not just as so many do, for the tipple!

It will already be becoming evident that judging is very much a matter of using certain senses to the full, namely those of sight, smell and taste, and in the next four chapters I will discuss them in detail.

Whenever possible, discuss the wine that you are drinking with a knowledgeable winemaker, if possible with a National Judge, If you make it known that one day you are hoping to take the examination of the A.W.N.G.J., you will find the judge most helpful and willing to share his knowledge with you. On each and every occasion that you find a new smell or taste in wine, re-smell and re-taste until you have fixed it in your memory for future use. This is what it is all about—Smelling, Tasting, Analysing and Remembering—S.T.A.R. This, of course, applies to both pleasant and unpleasant experiences. If you detect something new in a wine that you cannot recognise, where possible take the wine to someone and seek advice. Never be afraid to ask a question, even if it makes you appear foolish. It is better to be a fool for a few moments than one for the rest of your life!

You must learn to understand wine, and try to understand its complexities. No two wines are identical, although they may have very similar characteristics which are clearly identified. The best time for tasting wine is in the morning just before lunch. There is little merit in serious wine tasting immediately after a heavy meal, or when you are physically or mentally tired.

Chapter 3
Sight: Colour and Clarity

SIGHT

Sight is the first of the special senses to be used in the assessment of wine, for naturally we are deeply concerned with its colour and clarity.

In many ways the eye acts like a camera. Light enters it through a lens system which is called the iris, a diaphragm with a circular aperture called the pupil through which that light passes. The light falls not on to a film, as in a camera, but on to the retina, a complicated structure composed of light sensitive cells. This converts the light into nerve impulses which pass along the optic nerve to the brain. On receiving the sensory impulses, the brain sends a message back to the muscles of the iris. If the light is weak, these muscles relax and permit the pupil to dilate, thus allowing more light to pass through. If the light is strong they contract, so reducing the size of the pupil.

The human eye can recognise between 130 and 150 different colours, the very first impressions one gets of a wine are visual. They include not only the shape and colour of the bottle, but the label, and the colour and clarity of the wine. We are conditioned, through habit, to associate certain types of commercial wine with specific bottles, e.g. we do not expect to find still wine in champagne bottles and we would be most surprised to find champagne in a claret bottle. With a few exceptions, dark bottles are mainly used for red wines and clear bottles for white ones. Notable exceptions are white Burgundies and hocks. Rosé wine may be found in either dark or clear bottles. In amateur winemaker shows, all wines are bottled in white, flint-glass bottles to facilitate the assessment of the colour and clarity of the wine.

Clarity and colour are two different things. Both are seen simultaneously but they should receive independent assessment. Experience tells us that a cloudy wine is usually a defective one, so even before tasting it one has begun to form an opinion. A deposit in a commercial red wine is not necessarily a fault. Many red wines have a high tannin content and are excessively astringent when young but they improve tremendously with age, depositing some of the tannin on to the bottom of the bottle. In a wine that has been bottled for a considerable time, the deposit will probably be wedge shaped and will adhere firmly to the bottom of the bottle. It will not lift if the wine is carefully decanted. A deposit in a white wine is always a fault, except that of tartrates which will not affect the wine unless disturbed when pouring. However, for the purpose of exhibition in a wine show, A HAZE OR DEPOSIT IN ANY WINE IS CONSIDERED A FAULT.

HAZES

Hazes in wine originate from various sources. They are most commonly found in young, unpolished wines, and are due in this case to suspended yeast cells and cellular matter. Such wines usually have a milky appearance and invariably, have a yeasty nose and a yeast flavour. In young grape wines, or wines to which tartaric acid has been added, the milky appearance may be due to the precipitation of potassium bitartrate (argol). Crystals of this may be observed on the bottom of the bottle.

Another common haze is that caused by suspended pectin. This haze is not apparent when the wine is held before a bright light but is better seen in a diffused light. Pectin haze may not affect the palate impression to any great degree but it is not pleasing to the eye.

Wine infected by lactobaccili often has a silky, shimmering appearance when the bottle is rotated in the light. A wine with an advanced infection will have a thick oily consistency but it is extremely unlikely that this disorder will be found in a show wine.

CLARITY

The clarity of a wine is the first indication of its quality, for a really clear wine is free from suspended or precipitated matter. There are varying degrees of clarity:

1. Starbright or Brilliant

This refers to a wine of the highest possible degree of clarity. The wine scintillates. Sometimes referred to as a well polished wine.

2. Clear

This is the degree of clarity into which most wines fall. The wine is free from deposit or haze but lacks the final polish of a starbright one.

3. Dull or Slightly Hazy

The wine has a definite haze but is not cloudy.

4. Cloudy

The wine has a heavy haze which is generally accompanied by a deposit. This condition may indicate a young wine that has not cleared or an infected one produced by one or more spoilage organisms. It could also be found in a recently blended wine. Such wines often go cloudy and throw a deposit.

Small particles of pulp or other matter such as filter material are sometimes found on the bottom of the bottle. These are commonly called "floaters". This description arose because the particles float easily when the bottle is sharply rotated. These wines can be classified under section three or four, according to the amount of precipitation present.

A metallic haze may be found in a wine that has been fermented or stored in a metal container other than stainless steel. Dissolved metal in a wine, other than aluminium, can be toxic.

If the wine turns hazy when chilled, the haze is probably due to protein coming out of solution. This haze will probably disappear when the wine is brought into a warmer atmosphere.

Deposit that has a cottony appearance is probably due to contamination by lactobaccilli.

A haze in a wine made from grain, or in which grain has been incorporated, may be due to starch.

COLOUR

The colour of a wine is an important factor in its assessment. A wine with the wrong colour for its class can be instantly rejected, i.e. a red wine in a class for white wines. A wine with a poor colour and a haze would give such a poor first impression that it would start the evaluation at a very great disadvantage.

The experienced eye can assess a great deal from the colour of the wine.

A white wine with a dark amber colour is usually oxidised. This applies equally to a red wine with an amber hue. Raisins used in the production of wine will give it a characteristic colour.

A rosé wine of faded pink colour is usually indicative of a blend of white and red wine, rather than a true rosé, i.e. wine fermented on the pulp of red ingredients for a limited time.

Red wine made from elderberries or blackberries with a dense colour will usually be bitter and astringent due to its high tannin content.

Red wine with a violet hue is usually young. As the wine matures, the violet hue will disappear. Blended wines can also have a deep red colour.

If a red wine has turned amber, oxidation or long storage in a cask should be suspected. A thin amber colour, coupled with a watery appearance in a red table wine, may mean that the wine has outlived its life and has "gone over the top".

An amber colour in a red table wine that has aged is sometimes called an "onion peel colour" or "the eye of the partridge", In a dessert wine, this is called "tawny".

It is extremely difficult to classify accurately the various colours found in wines. The subject has been debated at length by many experienced practitioners of our hobby but, so far, no satisfactory solution has been found. Judges of honey use coloured glasses for assessing the colour of exhibition honey. This is a fairly simple test as all exhibition honey falls into three classes—light, medium and dark. Even so, a set of strips is fairly expensive. To produce a set of similar strips as a standard for colour assessment in wines, would be extremely difficult and the cost would be prohibitive.

Generally speaking, wines are classified into white, rosé, red and tawny. These basic colours are again subdivided into hues.

WHITE

Pale Straw—Most table wines fall into this category. It is the lightest shade of white wine. Sometimes it contains a hint of green.

Medium Straw—A very light wine, a little darker than pale straw colour. Many table wines are of this colour.

Light Golden—A much darker shade than the two previous classifications. Usually found in the sweeter type of table wine, but also found in dry white wine that has been stored in the bottle for several years.

Dark Golden—Many of the heavier, sweeter wines fall into this category. Where the Show Schedule states "white or golden" as the colour classification, all the colours so far mentioned should be accepted.

RED

Red wines are difficult to classify. There are numerous shades of red ranging from pale pink to deep red. Furthermore, the variety of red fruit used in winemaking, apart from grapes, will give their own characteristic hue to a wine. For example, sloes, damsons, plums, elderberries etc. Broadly speaking, red wines can be classified as follows:

Pale Pink—This is the lowest tint of red in a wine. It is really too faint for a rosé wine, although many such wines find their way to the show bench. This colour usually indicates a blend of red and white wines.

Medium Pink—This is the colour to aim for in a rosé wine. True rosé colour can only be obtained by a short pulp fermentation on the red ingredient. Rosé wine, if exposed to daylight for long periods, will darken and assume a brown tint. Some commercial rosé wines can have an orange hue. This is due to the variety of grapes used in its production.

Bottom Red—This colour is too high for a rosé, but not deep enough for a red wine. Many such wines are entered in classes for red wines but they seldom win prizes. This colour usually means a low wine extract and a lack of natural astringency. As a result, they do not stand up to better balanced wines. If such a wine did reach the short list, and was equal in overall impression to a wine with a good robe or colour, the latter would receive the better placing.

Medium Red—Most red table wines fall into this category. The wine has a good depth of colour. Many sweet and dessert wines also have this colour.

Deep Red—Young wines often have a purple or violet hue, particularly wines prepared from black grapes, fresh elderberries and bilberries. This colour can be very attractive but if large quantities of fruit have been used in the must, the colour may indicate excessive astringency. If the hue is only of moderate intensity, it will disappear as the wine matures and the wine will then assume a medium red colour. Wines which have been blended often have a deep red colour. Many of the red ingredients used in home winemaking have unstable pigments. Such wine will not retain its colour over long storage periods and the wine will discolour to a dark amber colour. Wine made from beetroots is a typical example. Red wines which are exposed to air will oxidise and turn amber, as will red wine stored for a long time in a cask.

Light to Medium Amber—These wines, usually referred to as tawny wines, may derive their colour from the basic ingredients. For example, dried rose hip shells or tea, but a tawny colour usually indicates a wine that has been exposed to the air unduly and as a result, large amounts of acetaldehyde have been formed. Most sweet sherries fall into this colour range. The description "tawny" in commercial wines is usually confined to Port.

So far, the colour of home-made wine has been related to the colour of commercial wines. Where home-made wines are made for a special purpose, for instance table wines etc., what better method than to compare their colour with such wines? However, does the colour of commercial wines cover the whole spectrum of wines made in the home? Obviously not. Many basic ingredients used in home-made wine production have their own characteristic hues and there will be no commercial equivalent. How then are such wines assessed and placed in regards to colour? One thing is obvious, where a show schedule stipulates a definite colour range for a class of wines, for instance "Fruit Wine, Red, Dry"—a wine with a blackish blue colour made from plums—would be out of class.

In short, so far as exhibition wine classes are concerned, the competitor wishing to enter those classes must produce the type of wine acceptable under the show classification.

Chapter 4

Smell: Bouquet and aroma

Of the three senses with which we are principally concerned—sight, smell and taste—that of smell is perhaps the most important to the wine judge. So much so that there is some truth in the old quip that "a beer drinker judges with his eyes, a winedrinker with his nose". Certainly one's first smell of a wine often tells all, even to the extent as to whether it is sound or not, and whether it is likely to prove good, bad or indifferent.

So a keen and accurate sense of smell is indispensable to a would-be wine judge.

How does it operate?

The interior of the nose is incompletely divided on each side, into four compartments, placed one above the other. The lower three serve as air passages. The olfactory receptors, which are comprised of spindle-shaped cells, are embedded in a small patch of mucous membrane situated on each wall of the uppermost compartment. This is a blind pocket from which the main air currents are excluded. This area, which is an adult measures about 500 sq. millimetre, is called the olfactory epithelium.

If one is suffering from a common cold there is

first of all an increase in sensitivity, followed by a temporary loss of smell. This is due firstly to the impairment of air circulation, and secondly to the surface area of the olfactory epithelium being covered by a layer of mucus which prevents penetration of the dissolved odoriferous substances. As the air passes clear, and the mucus disperses, the sense of smell returns.

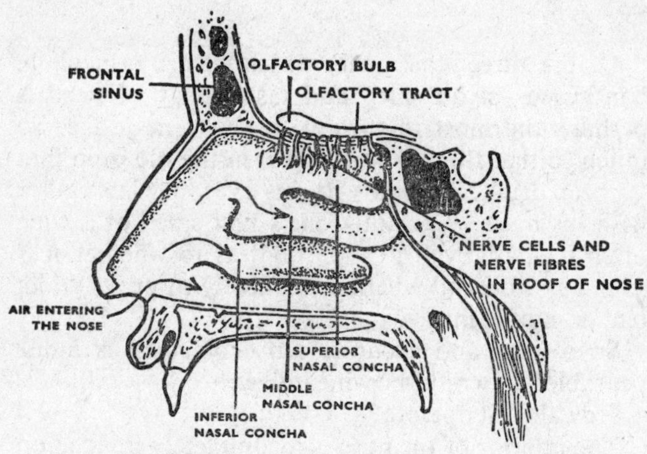

Scheme showing the nerve cells and fibres of the olfactory nerve in the roof of the nose.

Fig. 1

Smell is a chemical sense and the receptors respond to chemical stimuli. Flavour substances must be volatile in order to be smelt. They are volatilised quickly when warmed, so when wine is warmed in the mouth, its flavour particles will be more readily released than from a cold wine which is smelled in the glass. Both sensations are registered by the same nerve cells in the nose.

We smell substances by convection or diffusion. Air containing vapourised substances must be carried to the olfactory nerves either by diffusion or convection currents, set up when inspired air meets the warmer air within the nose. When we wish to smell some particular scent we inspire sharply, or "sniff". This sharp indrawing of the cooler outside air creates ascending convection currents which convey the flavour or scent particles to the sensitive area.

The flavour substances are partly dissolved in the mucosa, warmed by the mouth tissues and vaporised. The volatile particles then rise to the back of the nose and so reach the centre of smell. Enough volatile matter must penetrate for it to be stimulated. If the

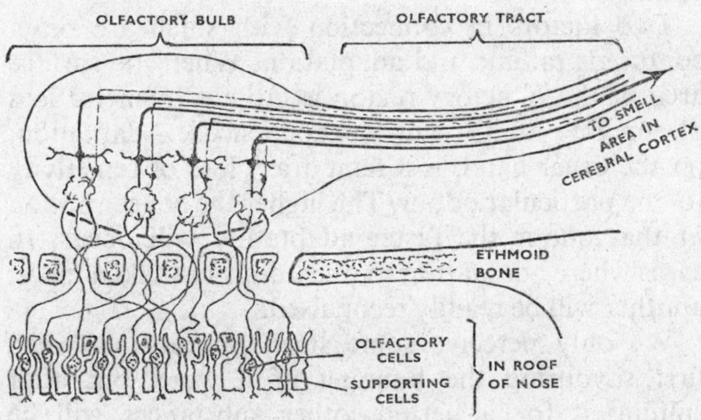

A magnified impression of the nerve cells and fibres in the roof of the nose, also showing the olfactory bulb and olfactory nerve tract.

Fig. 2

concentration is below a certain threshold level, no stimulus will occur.

The sense of smell is extremely sensitive, much more so than that of taste.

The olfactory region does two things. Firstly, it recognises the odoriferous substances conveyed to it by the nose—the **bouquet.** Secondly, it distinguishes substances directed to it after they have been warmed and volatilised in the mouth—**the aroma.**

The aroma is an integral part of any flavour and many of the so-called taste impressions are in, fact, olfactory ones. As will be seen, there are only four basic tastes, all other gradations are mixtures or those of smell. These may vary from extremely pleasant to the positively offensive ones. This can be demonstrated by the inability to taste when the nose is obstructed, and the sense of smell unable to operate.

Two factors in connection with smell are often confused; fatigue and adaptation. When the surface area of the olfactory region is fatigued, general loss of smelling ability will be experienced. Adaptation, on the other hand, is a temporary loss of sensitivity to one particular odour. The higher the concentration of that odour the faster adaptation will occur. In cases where adaptation to one odour has taken place, another will be readily recognised.

We only perceive some smell impressions when first savouring the bouquet of a wine, but after sniffing it for a period, other substances will be easily distinguished.

For example; if a wine contains two similar odoriferous substances at varying concentrations, the weaker smell will at first be masked by the stronger one, but as adaptation to the stronger smell takes place, the weaker odour will become noticeable.

Pasteur divided the odour of wine into three categories:

Primary odours which exist in the fruit; Secondary ones derived from fermentation; Tertiary odours developed during aging.

We tend to divide odours into pleasant or unpleasant ones. Our reaction to any odour is influenced by past experiences, it may conjure up a memory of a pleasant or unpleasant nature. Some smells may, therefore, be acceptable to one person but quite disagreeable to another.

PLEASANT ODOURS

These may be described in wine as:

Vinous—A wine should smell like a wine and not like a cordial.

Fruity—The fruity smell of wine, with one or two exceptions, is related to its age. Young wines usually have a fruity smell but this odour is replaced by other volatile substances produced by chemical changes during the maturing process. A wine may have both a fruity and vinous smell.

Varietal or Distinct—A wine naturally derives much of its smell from its basic ingredient i.e. elderflower, raspberry, rose petal etc. This is quite acceptable provided the smell is in balance with the rest of the bouquet.

Mature—The smell of a mature wine is full, rounded, soft and harmonious. The flavour components produced in a well and carefully matured wine will be pleasant and agreeable. A white wine matured for a number of years in a bottle may acquire a "honey" characteristic due to the action of a lactobaccillus. This odour is acceptable provided the wine has not developed a caramel smell.

UNPLEASANT ODOURS

Unpleasant odours in wine are more numerous:

Hydrogen Sulphide—Described as a smell of rotten eggs. This gas is formed when excess sulphur, which is applied to the growing grapes to control mildew, gets into the fermentation vessel, especially in a must with a high acid content. This smell may be confused with that of Ethyl Sulphide.

Earthy—What is known in Germany as "Erdgeschmack". In grape wine, this will only become apparent when the wine is warmed in the mouth. It can also occur in some wines made from root vegetables.

Mousey—This odour is usually associated with wine spoiled by lactobaccilli. A number of other odours are sometimes mistaken for mousiness. The best way to confirm one's suspicions is to rub a little of the wine briskly between the palms of the hands. The heat generated will release the characteristic odour. If the wine IS mousey, it will be necessary to wash one's hands well with soap and hot water as the smell of this compound is very persistent. Some people are unable to recognise this smell.

Oxidation—This odour is usually considered a fault. Only in wines such as sherries and heavy dessert wines is it regarded as a desirable characteristic. The term "bottle sickness" refers to a temporary oxidation after bottling. The odour is due to the formation of excessive acetaldehyde produced in the wine by its being exposed to the air.

Woody or Casky—This odour is found in wine which has been left too long in a cask, or by using a new unconditioned cask. In many red table wines, a trace of this odour is acceptable. It is always a fault in a white table wine.

Green—This smell is very distinctive and should not be confused with oxidation. It is usually associaated with an acidic wine. In grape wine it is due to the use of unripe fruit. The Portuguese wine Vinho Verde is a good example; this wine is made from grapes which are grown "high" and as a result, contain more acid and less sugar than those which are pruned low. It is very often found in home-made wines, both red and white, and is probably due also to the use of unripe fruit. A lot of our indigenous fruits have only an external appearance of ripeness in the early ripening stage.

Yeasty—Young wines often have a pronounced odour of yeast. This will usually disappear after storage and one or two efficient rackings.

Lees—If the wine is left in contact with the lees for too long, it may acquire a very unpleasant odour— "lees odour".

Acetic—This well known odour is usually termed as vinegary. It indicates an excess of acetic acid produced either by contamination by Acetobacter or oxidation of higher alcohols. In the latter case, the amount of acetic acid produced will remain constant. If formed by contamination the wine will increase in acidity until it is vinegar.

Mouldy—This odour is produced when the must has not been sufficiently sterilised and mould spores from the fruit are still active. Wine stored in a stale or mould infected jar or cask will, of course, acquire a mouldy smell.

Almond—Wines made from stone fruits sometimes have this smell. It is caused by leaching of the kernels after excessively long pulp fermentation.

Filter Pad—In wines that have been badly filtered, a "cardboard" smell and taste is sometimes discernible.

Pulp—This characteristic odour is found in wines which have been fermented too long on the pulp. It is sometimes accompanied by an acrid smell.

Sulphite—An excess of sulphite in a wine is often referred to as a smell. Its action, however, is on the common chemical sense and not on the smell receptors.

Baked—Wine made from inferior grape concentrate often has this baked or cooked odour. It may also be found in a fruit wine in which the ingredients have been boiled.

Stagnant—A smell reminiscent of stagnant water, probably due to a bacterial infection.

Lactic—Sometimes described as a goaty odour or sour milk smell.

Corked—It is estimated that only one bottle of wine in 10,000 is corked. This smell is usually due to mould spores on the cork and is usually found in bottles which have excessive ullage. The wine may be infected by bacteria.

Raisin—A characteristic smell found in wines when raisins have been used in their production.

Caramel—This term may be used in conjunction with either baked or raisin wines. They both have a burnt sugar or caramel characteristic.

Brandy—This odour may be found in wines that

have fermented at too high a temperature. Such usually wines have an excess of fusel oil.

Foxy—Is only encountered in wines made from the Concord grape in America. Whether this is acceptable or unacceptable depends on individual taste.

Cheesy—A definite smell, reminiscent of cheese. Probably due to a lactobaccillus infection.

Hessian—Wines which have been pressed through hessian may acquire this smell from the cloth.

All the above odours can occur singly or as mixtures. It is, therefore, sometimes very difficult to pinpoint exactly whence the off odour comes as the quantities involved may be very small.

This chapter seems to have become willy-nilly a list of the unpleasant odours one can sometimes encounter in wines. I should perhaps redress the balance by emphasising that many wines of which one savours the bouquet will be adequately fruity, vinous, and wholly agreeable, so much so that one postpones tasting to savour the delights of the bouquet all the more. It is, when all is said and done, one of the wine drinker's principal pleasures.

Chapter 5
Taste: Flavour and Texture

TASTE

Nature endowed man with a sense of taste, not so much to allow him the sensory enjoyment of food and drink as to enable him to reject some foods which are harmful. Nevertheless, the sense of taste probably provides man with more enjoyment during his whole life than any other sense, for whereas other senses slowly deteriorate, that of taste will continue to provide enjoyment even in old age, particularly if one is a lover of wine. It has been suggested that taste enables the body to obtain food deficiencies. This is achieved by reducing the threshold of taste buds so that they are stimulated by even a low concentration of the missing substance. For instance, lack of salt will produce a desire for it and salty foods are eaten with relish.

As our knowledge increases about the chemical stimuli of the taste buds and the manner by which the brain processes the information fed to it, so shall we have a better understanding of the sense of taste.

The taste receptors, or "taste buds", are found in the walls of the papillae on the surface of the tongue. Taste sensitivity is greater at the tip, on the sides and base of the tongue, and this is where most of the taste buds are to be found. There are two types of

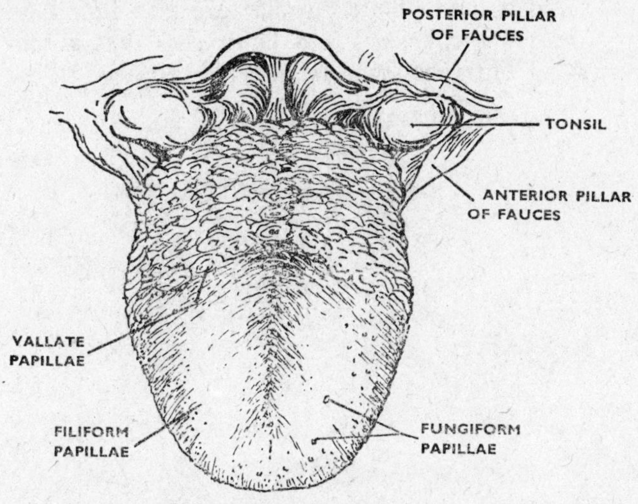

The tongue showing the papillae

Fig. 3

papillae in man which have taste-active cells; they are the Fungiform and Circumvallate.

Fungiform papillae are mushroom shaped, approximately 1.0 mm. in diameter and 1.0 mm. to 1.5 mm. high. Their density is highest at the tip and on the sides of the tongue. They vary in number from 150 to 400.

Circumvallate papillae are arranged in a V form at the base of the tongue. They derive their name from their odd shape, something like a small wall surrounded by a trench. They are quite large, 2.0 mm. high and they number from seven to fifteen.

Each papilla consists of a bunch of taste buds. In adults, the number of buds per papilla varies from 30 to 500, the average number being 250, hence the difference in individuals to taste stimulus. Some

scattered circumvalliate papillae are also found ou
the pharynx, epiglottis and larynx, so that a sensation of bitterness may be experienced deep in the
throat.

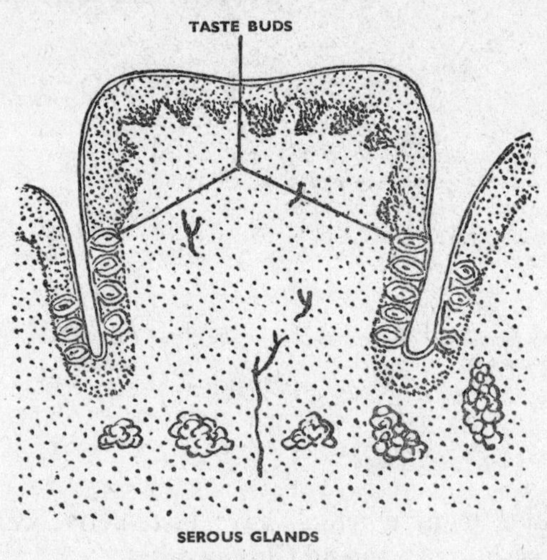

A taste bud magnified.   Fig. 4

There are four sets of taste buds which give the
sensation of sweet, sour, salt and bitter tastes. A
sweet taste is given by a substance such as sugar, a salt
taste by sodium chloride, a sour taste by acid such as
citric, tartaric acid etc., and a bitter taste by quinine,
tannin and other substances. A taste bud is stimulated
by chemical changes in its environment. Certain
parts of the tongue are more responsive than others
to the various substances. Saltiness and sweetness
are recognised by buds on the tip of the tongue but a
little sweetness may also be sensed on the sides. Most
of the taste buds which respond to sourness are found

on the sides of the tongue, bitterness is recognised by buds at the back. There are very few, if any, buds on the upper and centre surface of the tongue although a few may be found in the mucosa of the lower palate. In children, buds are found in the front and sides of the palate and these mostly respond to sweetness.

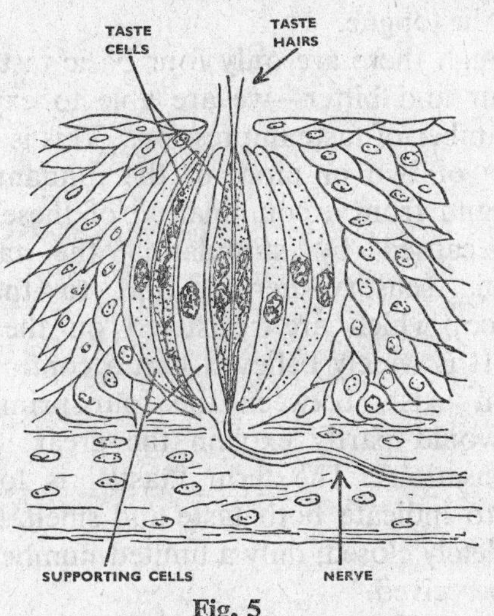

Fig. 5

There is a variation of taste impressions amongst individuals which is due in part to the difference in the enzymatic structure of the saliva. Some people are "taste blind" and can only perceive certain tastes, in the same way that a person who is colour blind has a limited colour spectrum. Taste blindness does not prevent a person from having very definite views of what they do taste; they also know what they like and dislike. Ethoxyphenyl thiorea is an example of a substance whose taste stimulus varies from person to person. About one third of the population are unable to taste this substance, the remaining two thirds find that it has a bitter taste. The ability to taste it is inherited according to Mendelian laws. If one takes a little sodium salicylate—a sweet, bitter substance—into the mouth, the bitter part is not noticed until after the substance has passed over the back of the tongue.

Although there are only four basic tastes—sweet, salt, sour and bitter—we are able to experience a great number of taste impressions. This is due to the blending of two or more of the fundamental sensations and from a combination of these with sensations caused by stimulating the tactile and cutaneous sensory nerves, and to the volatile substances which are registered on the olfactory nerves. It is widely believed that a continuous taste spectrum exists between the four primary tastes which would partly explain the great number of taste sensations. The term "taste" is loosely employed to indicate both taste and smell. If the nose is completely closed, only a limited number of tastes will be perceived.

This is easily demonstrated by completely closing the nose, thus eliminating smell, and being fed blindfold with a little minced turnip, onion, apple and carrot in turn. They will all taste the same, slightly sweet but nothing more.

The sense of taste is fairly discriminating. For instance, sweet and acid substances can be tasted simultaneously. This is illustrated by the over acid, over sweet wine which is often exhibited as a dry wine. The trained, experienced palate can recognise both taste impressions separately, whereas to the inexperienced palate the masking effect of the acid on the sugar gives the impression of dryness. The reaction of a wine judge to the various taste substances will depend to a large extent on the training of his palate and experience in wine tasting. The more experienced judge will have a lower threshold level for the substances found in wine and, as a result, will be able to form an opinion more quickly than a less experienced taster. He will also be able to differentiate more easily between wines of near equal quality.

The threshold of a taste substance is defined as the smallest amount necessary to produce a response from the taste receptors. Any substance has a detection and recognition level. If a small amount of acid is added to a neutral tasting solvent, a point is reached where the substance is detected but the taster is unable to recognise what the substance is. By increasing the amount of acid in solution, it becomes recognisable.

Some substances modify tastes. An example is the fruit of the plant *Synsepalum Dulcificum* found in Nigeria, which modifies the taste so that sour substances are tasted as sweet.

The saliva plays a very important part in the recognition of taste substances. It forms a solution with solids so that they can be recognised by taste and smell. Solids which contain no water have very little smell, and dry solids have no taste. If a lump of sugar is placed on the centre of the tongue, there will be no taste impression until the saliva has dissolved the lower surface and the solution has spread over the surface of the tongue. Wine is diluted by the saliva, which also changes its temperature.

The flow of saliva is stimulated by the presence of food or wine in the mouth. The saliva flow may also be stimulated by the sight, smell or thought of food or wine. The first instance is an unconditional reflex and the second a conditional one.

Pavlov, the Russian physiologist (1910) found that the ringing of the midday bells at St. Petersburgh—now Leningrad—caused salivation amongst his experimental dogs. This was the usual feeding time and a conditional reflex had developed between the presentation of food and the ringing of the bells. The chiming of the bells, without food, produced salivation once the reflex had been established. How often have we heard the term "mouth watering"? When we taste wine for the first time, there is a secretion of saliva due to the stimulation of the taste buds. This is a simple, unconditional reflex.

When more experience has been gained in wine drinking, one associates the appearance and smell of wine with the taste and there may then be a secretion of saliva without actually taking the wine into the mouth. A pathway has been established in the brain between the centre of sight and smell and the salivary centre. This is a conditional reflex. In other words, the visual and olfactory stimuli set up impulses which act on the salivary centre without stimulation of the taste buds, "making the mouth water".

Whilst taste is a mixture of taste and aroma sensations, there are a number of substances which are olfactorily neutral, but which have specific flavours i.e. citric acid, and the various sugars. As the various taste cells are only able to respond to one type of stimulus, those which respond to sugar will not respond to acid or bitterness, and those which react to bitter substances will not respond to sweet ones. As the various taste buds are situated in different parts of the mouth, it is essential that the wine should be in contact with them all simultaneously so that an overall impression may be registered.

Sweetness is the first taste to be recognised when the wine passes over the tip of the tongue. It is associated with the various sugars, saccharin, glycerin and other substances.

As the wine enters the mouth, it comes into contact with the cells at the sides of the tongue which register sourness but a few of the cells also register sweetness. Sourness is associated with the two groups of acids, mineral and organic. Mineral acids such as nitric, hydrochloric and sulphuric give a slight impression of sourness when diluted, but the organic acids, those which we are concerned with in wine, may have other tastes. For instance, citric acid will give both sweet and sour impressions.

The last sensation is of bitterness and comes when the wine reaches the back of the tongue. Bitterness is linked with tannin. Hops and quinine have a bitter taste. One pit into which many amateurs fall is the confusion between bitterness and acidity, yet the two are quite different. The sensation of bitterness, caused by excess tannin, is accompanied by a rough sensation in the mouth—tannin "grips" the teeth. This roughness is absent with excess acid and no amount of acid dilution will affect the bitterness.

One of the main difficulties of a wine judge is being able to express his gustatory experience, in terms that will mean something specific, and in terms that can be understood by the average winedrinker. Taste and smell are subjective impressions and as such, are sometimes difficult to describe. Terms like "a pleasant wine", "charming", "graceful", "not a table wine", "not a good wine", etc., mean very little and unless the term means something specific, it is better not to use it. Some general terms have specific meanings. These may usefully be employed in the description of wine. They are as follows:

Acid—**There are a number of different acids in wine.** Some are beneficial and others, when in excess, are detrimental. Wine which is deficient in acid is flat and flabby. Too much acid will make the wine hard and unpleasant.

Astringent—Related to the tannin content. Red wines have a higher astringency than white wines. Too much astringency leaves the mouth rough and dry and its effect may be felt on the teeth, also on the after-taste, which is bitter.

Acetic—Contamination of the wine by acetobacter will turn it to vinegar. There is no cure.

Lees—A very unpleasant taste caused by leaving the wine too long on its sediment. Very seldom found in commercial wine but a common fault in wine made in the home by inexperienced winemakers.

Balanced—A wine is said to be balanced when all the components, acid, sugar, tannin, alcohol, flavour etc., are in perfect harmony, each with the other.

Sweet—Indicating a high sugar residue. Whilst this is desirable in a dessert wine, it is in our field usually reckoned a fault in table wines. If the wine is low in acid, the sweet sensation may be very unpleasant, even to the point of inducing nausea.

Body—The depth of fullness experienced when the wine is in the mouth. The sensation is largely produced by the extract of wine but sugar, glycerin and alcohol are contributory factors. A wine with high alcohol usually has a high wine extract.

Caramel—Often found in wine made from concentrates, cooked ingredients and brown sugar. Also found in some wines which are over the top.

Dry—Indicating a wine in which the sugar residue is below threshold level with a low glycerol content.

Fruity—A flavour derived mainly from the basic fruit ingredients. Usually indicating a youthful wine but generally speaking, it will disappear as the wine matures. One or two wines will hold their fruity flavour over many years; raspberry and blackberry are examples. A mature wine may also have a fruity taste imparted by the formation of esters.

Flat or Flabby—Indicating a wine which is low in acidity or stringency, uninteresting and lacking bite.

Delicate—A light, sensitive wine.

Fusel Oil—A combination of higher alcohols giving the wine a "hot" feel.

Depth—The flavour gives the impression of having layers.

Full Bodied—Describes a wine which is rich and full in the mouth.

After Taste—May be pleasant or unpleasant. A pleasant after taste leaves the mouth fresh and tingling. The flavour lingers on the palate after the wine has been swallowed which indicates that the wine has the right amount of acidity and a good balance. An unpleasant after taste may leave a bitter sensation or a nasty taste in the mouth which may last for quite a long time.

Watery—The wine shows a lack of acidity, alcohol and flavour, and lacks quality.

Mousey—A very descriptive term. Not everyone is able to recognise this fault which is due to the action of lacto baccilli and the subsequent formation of chemical compounds such as acetamide and acrolien.

Oxidised—A very common fault in wine made in the home. May be caused by a film yeast or, more commonly, by exposing wine to air over periods of storage. If the oxidation is slight as in bottle sickness in a freshly bottled wine, the wine will recover. If the wine has been subjected to longer periods of exposure, the colour will darken and in the case of a red wine, the pigment will go brown. Oxidation leads to the formation of excessive quantities of acetaldehyde and if the exposure is prolonged, secondary products may be formed, giving the wine a taste similar to metallic.

Pulpy—Wines which are fermented too long on the pulp may acquire a very distinctive off flavour. If the basic ingredient was a seeded fruit, i.e. raspberry, blackberry, loganberry or Boysenberry, then the flavour will include an acrid sensation on the palate. There may also be excessive bitterness.

Green—Usually associated with wine made from unripe fruit. Such wines are acidulous. A green taste is sometimes mistaken for an oxidised taste but the latter is not necessarily acid.

Woody—Wine stored for too long in a cask will acquire a woody or casky flavour. A trace of woodiness is acceptable in a red table wine but it is always a fault in a dry white table wine.

Chapter 6
Other Senses: Other Impressions—

In addition to the special senses already dealt with, there are others directly concerned with wine evaluation, although it may not at first be realised that they play any part.

Hearing—The sense of hearing can indirectly but greatly influence the less experienced wine taster. A taster, having reached a conclusion about a wine, on overhearing a more experienced taster giving his opinion on the same wine, may be influenced by these comments and reverse his own assessment accordingly. By the same token, if another wine taster expresses his views about a wine before the taster has evaluated it, the comments of the first taster can influence the opinion of the second.

Common Chemical Sense—This sense involves the nerve endings of the Trigeminal nerve which are situated in the eyes, mouth and nose and respond to a number of irritants. When these nerve endings are stimulated, watering of the eyes, sneezing and choking can take place. The coolness of inhaled menthol is recognised by this sense. The common chemical sense performs independently from the olfactory sense. A typical example is the irritation caused by smelling a wine with a high sulphur dioxide content. The high alcohol content of thin table wines or other wines with a high alcohol content and a low wine extract, will stimulate the nerve endings thus giving a hot sensation on the palate. Fusel oil and acetaldehyde may give the same responses.

Tactile Sense—The mucous membranes of the mouth and nose contain nerves which respond to tactile or touch sensations. Other cutaneous impressions are registered by nerve endings in the muscles of the tongue. It is this sense which responds to stimulus by the residual gas in petillant and sparkling wines.

Other sensations which are registered include the high body of dessert wines, the thin feel of light table wines, the rawness and harshness of some young wines, and the smoothness of mature wines. The oily feel of ropy wines is a tactile sensation. The inhomogeneity of a freshly sweetened wine is probably recognised by the senses of taste and touch. The sense of taste registers the sweetness, and the sense of touch that the sweetness is not an integral part of the whole, but something that has not yet blended with the other components.

Chapter 7
Equipment for Judging

EQUIPMENT

Certain items of equipment are essential for the judging of wine, but the wise judge will keep this equipment down to the essentials. The only essential items are:

For Judging Still Wine
Six tasting glasses
Spittoon
Receptacle for water (i.e. plastic bucket or bowl)
Glass cloth
Marking board
Marking sheets
Pen or pencil
Corkscrew
Palate cleanser

Optional
Plastic rack for draining glasses
Candle or torch

Six tasting glasses are advisable in order to have sufficient glasses to make the final selection. Many wine judges include a plastic draining rack to hold their glasses after rinsing, as this makes it unnecessary to dry them. The tasting glass is of primary impor-

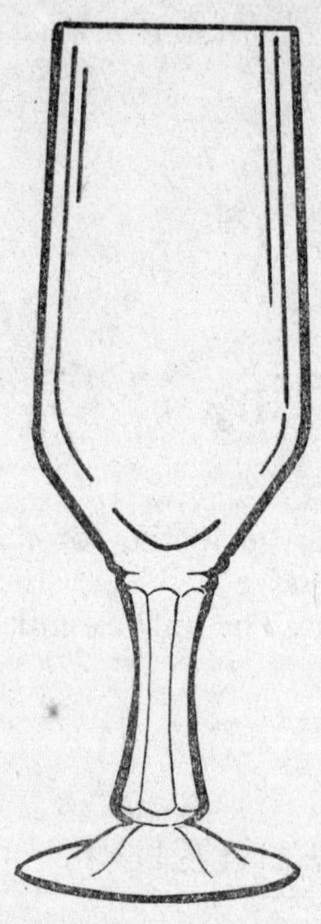

Fig 6

Recommended Ravenshead
tasting glass

Glass for sparkling
wines

The glass now officially recommended for winetasting by the International Organisation for Standardisation has the shape of an "elongated egg", rather than the tulip shape favoured by some tasters, and is ideal for the rapid and accurate appraisal of the bouquet. The dimensions are precisely laid down as follows: Capacity 215 mls., weight 155mm., height of cup 100 mm., diameter of cup at broadest part 65 mm., diameter at brim 46 mm., thickness of glass 0.8 mm., height of stem 55 m., diameter of stem 9 mm., diameter of foot 65 mm. The glass must be absolutely transparent and crystalline, and the brim carefully polished. There is only one snag, and that is that such a glass does not seem to be commonly available yet!

But a somewhat similar glass, and that which can be highly recommended, is the one above, made by Ravenshead Glass. It is cheap (35p), has a capacity of 5 oz. and is a stock line. Whilst the shape is not perfect in that the sides are not quite curved enough, it is probably the best available.

For sparkling wines a "flute" such as that on the right is recommended.

tance. The ideal glass for wine tasting should have the shape of an elongated egg, with a capacity of about six ounces. It should be crystal clear and thin walled. The brim of the glass should be polished; an unpolished edge may impart a physical distraction to the lips, and thus affect the objective response of the judge.

To judge sparkling wines, a different type of glass is used. The judge will require three or four tall stemmed, tulip shaped glasses of about six ounces capacity, also a pair of pliers or wire cutters for cutting the retaining wires.

Try a test yourself. Pour some wine from the same bottle into four glasses of different size and shape. Now savour the bouquet. The experienced nose will detect subtle differences of depth. Carry the test one stage further and vary the volume of wine in each glass. Now smell the wine, and you will notice a marked difference between the samples. I should add that the response to this test varies according to the wine being tested. For example, a clean wine with a little bouquet will not give such a marked response as that from a wine with a more volatile nose, accompanied by slight undertones.

It follows, therefore, that when judging one wine against another it is necessary, in order to give a fair assessment, to have an equal volume of wine from each bottle in identical glasses.

After use, the tasting glass should be rinsed, preferably under running water. Ideally, the glass should then be rinsed with distilled water and finally with the wine to be tasted. In practice, this is rarely possible and the judge has to compromise.

There are, however, several points to remember.

Detergents should *not* be used in cleaning glasses: they have a smell of their own; furthermore, if tasting sparkling wines or beers, the detergent will effectively kill the head.

Drying cloths are slowly falling into disuse and the method is to let the glasses drain. A drying cloth may impart a smell to the glass and there is also danger of particles of the fabric adhering to the glass.

The spittoon is used for receiving the ejected wine after tasting. A polythene container and small funnel are quite useful, but any empty bottle and funnel will do. The spittoon should be emptied before it gets too full. Eject the wine from your mouth into the spittoon with a sharp crisp motion. Never hold the spittoon under your nose for any length of time as the fumes will rise from it and accelerate smell fatigue. Both container and funnel should be well washed immediately after use.

A linen glass cloth is useful for the final drying of the glasses after judging and for general use during the tasting session.

A small polythene bucket can be used for holding the rinsing water for the glasses. If a judge is travelling by car, it is advisable to take a bucket as part of the judging equipment. Most of the Show Organisers provide washing up vessels but often there are not enough to go round, particularly if the wine section is part of a Horticultural Show, and held under canvas.

If the weather is warm, and if white wine is being judged, the rinsing water should be as cold as possible; in any case, it should always be cold. On the other hand, if red wine is being judged, and the weather is cold, it is better to use warm water.

AMATEUR WINEMAKERS' NATIONAL GUILD OF JUDGES

VENUE **BACTON SHOW**   DATE **6-8-76**

JUDGE **PERCY VEERANCE**   CLASS **14 RED DRY TABLE**

MARKING SHEET

EXB. No.	Presentation (2)	Clarity (4)	Bouquet (4)	Flavour Balance Quality (20) General Impression	Total (30)	EXB. No.	REMARKS
1	2	2	2	11	17	1	UNCLEAN NOSE. SLIGHT SED. – THIN. BITTER FAREWELL
2	2	3	3	16	25	2	A little harsh. YOUNG, WILL KEEP.
3	2	3	3	12	20	3	TOO FRUITY – ALCOHOL ++
4	2	3	1½	8	14½	4	? LEES ODOUR & FLAVOUR BITTER
5	N.A.S. DISQUALIFIED —					5	WRONG CORK!
6	2	4	3	9	18	6	THIN. WATERY. ? OVER-FILTERED
7	2	3	4	18	27	7	WELL-BALANCED
8	2	3	2	8	15	8	GREEN NOSE – over acid
9	2	2	2½	—	6½	9	'OFF' BOUQUET – TOO SWEET
10	2	—	—	—	2	10	V. HAZY. SULPHITE ++
11	2	3	3	15	23	11	Bit high in acid.
12	2	3	3	10	18	12	HARSH, ASTRINGENT, BITTER. Too much fruit
13	2	3	2	—	7	13	SWEET!
14	2	3	—	—	—	14	ACETIC!
15	2	3	3	—	8	15	STILL FERMENTING — CO_2.
16	2	2½	2	—	6½	16	SLIGHT PEARDROP BQT. Amyl acetate
17	2	3	4	18	27	17	HARMONIOUS AND AGREEABLE
18	DISQUALIFIED – Wrong class				(White wine).		
19	2	3	3	13	20	19	VERY FRUITY FLAVOUR HIGH, ALC. +
20	2	2	4	17	25	20	NICE TABLE WINE, SL. OVER-ACID
21	2	3	3	11	19	21	SLIGHTLY OVER-SWEET AND OVER-ACID
22	2	3	3	16	24	22	WELL-BALANCED BUT LACKS QUALITY
23	2	3	2½	13½	20½	23	GREEN NOSE, OVER-ACID
24	2	3	—	—	—	24	MOUSEY!
25	2	3	3	12	20	25	TOO YOUNG; NEEDS MATURING
26	2	1	1	8	12	26	SL. SED. OFF BQT. HARSH. BITTER
27	2	3	2	9	16	27	Unclean bqt. Bitter farewell.
28	2	3	3	17	25	28	A LITTLE OVER-ASTRINGENT.
29	2	2	2	10	16	29	OXIDISED
30	2	3	3	11	19	30	Fair balance, but thin.
				1ST.	17		
				2ND.	7		
				3RD.	20		
				4TH.	2		
				5TH.	28		

Always change the water before it gets too contaminated with wine. Make sure that the water has not been chlorinated recently. If the correct judging procedure is observed, i.e. the wine is smelled in the bottle before being poured into the tasting glass, acetified wine should never be poured into the glass. If, however, by mistake the glass does have acetified wine poured into it, it should then be thoroughly washed before being used again, and the rinsing water immediately changed.

The board supporting the marking sheet should be rigid, with a smooth surface. It should be a little larger than the average marking sheet, about 35 cm. × 22 cm. and have bulldog clip at the top for holding the paper.

The marking sheet should have a space at the top for the judge's name, the name of the venue, date and class to be judged. A space for the number of exhibits in the class is also useful. The remainder of the sheet is divided by horizontal and vertical lines into sections for (a) Exhibitor's number; (b) Marks for presentation (two points) (c) Clarity (four points); (d) Bouquet (four points); (e) Balance, quality and overall impression (20 points). The marks in brackets are those used by members of the Amatuer Winemakers National Guild of Judges and are based on the marks as used by judges at The International Wine Competition held at Budapest in 1964. However, any number of marks can be used. For example, presentation could be given 10 marks, clarity 15, bouquet 15 and overall impression 60, making a total of 100.

The wines are only marked by this mathematical system in order to make the task of selecting the "short list" easier. In practice, the system of the A.W.N.G.J. works very well; if the judge feels he needs more scope in his markings, he can always award half marks.

After the column for overall impression, comes one for the total of marks awarded. This is followed by a second column for the exhibitor's number and the remainder of the line is used for the comments of the judge. The reason for having a second column for the exhibitor's number is that the marking sheet can then be folded over for the "Judges at The Bar" session, after the judging. In this way, only the exhibitor's number and the remarks are visible. This prevents the exhibitor, or other persons, looking at the marks given to any wine. The uninformed exhibitor would probably receive an entirely wrong impression by observing the marks of a judge. A judge, therefore, should never leave his marked sheets behind after a judging session. However, there is no reason why he should not detach his marks from the sheet and leave his comments with the exhibitor's number behind, if so requested. This information could be left with the Show Secretary and would be available for those exhibitors who were unable to attend the "Judges at The Bar" session.

Perhaps a word of explanation is needed here about the "Judges at The Bar" session. This refers to the time set aside at a show when the exhibitor can ask the judge to give comments about his wine. The judge stands by the section of the wine show that he had judged, hence "Judges at The Bar". It does NOT, as some newcomers to the hobby seem to think, mean that all the judges gather at the bar to regale them- selves with liquid refreshment, although after tasting some of the wines, one could hardly blame them!

It is advisable to include one or two spare marking sheets. Marking sheets are usually provided at most of the larger shows but judges usually provide their own at the smaller shows. Marking sheets can be purchased from the Amateur Winemaker Publications Ltd., and members of the A.W.N.G.J. can obtain their own marking sheets from The Guild Supplies Officer—these sheets are embossed with The Guild crest.

It is advisable to take two pens to the judging session. It is useful to have one pen with a black felt nib as sometimes the Award Cards, which the judge has to sign, are glazed and it is difficult to write on them with a biro, but a felt pen will write quite easily on such a surface.

Although it is standard practice to use all-cork stoppers for wine exhibits, some corks are faulty and tend to break when being removed. For this reason the corkscrew comes in handy.

The palate would tire very quickly if subjected to continual tasting of wine without some palate cleansing. Judges vary in their choice of palate cleanser. Some like to eat a piece of apple and others a small piece of celery, bread or cheese. The latter is used less amongst experienced judges. Personally, I rinse my mouth with water after each tasting; this I then swallow as it serves the double purpose of removing traces of wine from my mouth and throat. I know of many judges who follow this practice. Cheese has a strong flavour of its own, and traces left in the mouth may affect the flavour of the wine. If I have tasted a wine with a strong off flavour, I do sometimes eat a piece of cheese and dry bread, but I always rinse my mouth well with water before sampling the next wine. Apple and celery also leave their own flavour on the palate. Dry bread is a useful palate cleanser when judging the heavier dessert wines with a high sugar residue. However, the mouth should again be rinsed with water before the next sample. Water alone has its effect on the taste buds and mouth tissues and, of course, varies from district to district. Some water is very hard and contains a lot of trace minerals, other water is soft. It is advisable to take a bottle of water from your own supply, as your palate will be attuned to its characteristics and the effect on your palate will be more neutral than that produced by water from another source.

Other items of equipment which a judge may find useful include a candle, or a small electric torch. Very occasionally, one finds a venue where the lighting is inadequate—a tented marquee during inclement weather is a typical example.

If you are judging at a show with composite exhibits, you may be invited to join a small panel to judge these. As many of the show schedules stipulate a maximum size for these exhibits, a tape measure would be useful.

In the early days of wine judging, it was not un-common for a judge to include a hydrometer in his equipment. I can remember one judge who included equipment for acid titration and iodine for a starch haze test! Today, the inclusion of such items would be regarded with amusement. By the uninitiated, a hydrometer may be regarded as a sensible piece of equipment but, although it will determine the presence and approximate quantity of sugar in a wine with a high gravity, it will only be a rough guide as to whether the wine is sweet or dry. The palate must be the deciding factor. It is generally assumed that a wine with a neutral reading i.e. 1.000 is a dry wine, as this is the reading of water without additives. There are many factors which affect the gravity reading of a finished wine, but I do not intend to go too deeply into these. They are fully covered in "Progressive Winemaking" by Peter Duncan and Bryan Acton. Nevertheless, I think a few words of explanation are necessary.

Wine contains, in addition to the residue of sugar, varying amounts of solids and glycerols formed as a by-product of fermentation. As alcohol has a lower specific gravity than water, its effect on the final gravity of the wine must also be considered. Wine made from a must which has been sterilised by the use of sulphite, will usually contain more glycerine than must sterilised by other methods. Glycerine has a smoothing effect on a harsh wine as it has a sweet taste and will, therefore, have its own effect on the overall impression of the wine. Glycerine will help to mask acidity and astringency and may give the impression of slight sweetness to a wine with a low sugar residue. So, you see, a hydrometer would not be of much value in determining the dryness of a wine.

In addition to the equipment already mentioned, it is essential for the judge to have a copy of the show schedule. He should read the rules very carefully before commencing to judge to familiarise himself with any local rules. For instance, the system of labelling the bottles may vary slightly from show to show.

Chapter 8
The Technique of Wine Tasting

It is essential when judging wine to be in good physical condition, for tiredness or mental stress can impair one's judgement. This should be borne in mind when the tasting is immediately preceded by a tedious car journey. A short rest should be taken before starting with the tasting.

Body temperature can also affect one's evaluation of wine. If you arrive at a venue feeling cold and chilly, try to obtain a warm drink of tea or coffee before commencing to judge. The average individual is unaware of the close connection between the nerves of the ears, nose, mouth and throat. For instance, a judge may have a slight ear infection and think this could not possibly affect his palate. On the contrary, a temporary but complete loss of taste on one side of the mouth can occur. I have experienced this, and know of other cases. In my case, the loss of sensation lasted for two days.

When tasting wine, the effect of the previous sample on the palate should be borne in mind, as this may unduly influence the impression of the wine being tasted. A wine with a subtle nose and delicate flavour could be underrated if it follows a wine with a robust bouquet and flavour. By the same token, the quality of a well balanced wine, preceded by a wine with excessive astringency, may not be fully appreciated. A white wine with a very high acid content can adversely influence the impression of a wine with the correct amount of acidity. A wine with a powerful off flavour will also affect the evaluation of the next sample. A good judge will, of course, be aware of these influences and act accordingly. For this reason, it is undesirable to hurry your tasting. Sufficient time should be allowed between samples for cleansing of the palate and allowing the taste receptors to recover from the previous tasting. Your memory will, of course, carry the impressions forward.

I have always maintained that it is of far greater importance for the wine judge to be able to differentiate between wines of near equal quality, than to tabulate accurately undesirable odours and flavours, and nothing has happened during the past 19 years I have been judging to alter this opinion. At the same time, a judge must be able to recognise the many imperfections of wines. This knowledge is, of course, obtained during his practical making of wine and wine drinking with his friends, and not just at the show bench, although there as well one is continually learning.

A large memory of subjective impressions of wine is not acquired overnight. It is the result of many years of hard work in tasting and re-tasting of many wines, both home-made and commercial, coupled with the practical experience gained over the years by making a lot of wine from many different ingredients. During my years of experimental winemaking, I had over 50 different wines in my cellar and although that number has now been reduced to about a dozen, the knowledge gained and recorded during those years is of inestimable value.

Commercial wines are made almost exclusively from grapes. The different types of wine are produced by the variety of grapes used, the type of yeast and production method, and by careful blending. The climatic and soil conditions prevailing in the area of growth also impart to the wine a definite characteristic. However, the constant factor in all the still and sparkling wines will always be the unmistakable flavour of the grape. How are we then able to evaluate the many distinctive bouquets and flavours of wines made from a variety of basic ingredients in the home?

If we are going to use commercial wine as a yardstick, where do we find a wine against which to evaluate a parsnip or wheat wine, and what about a wine made from rosehips? The progressive winemaker will probably argue—why bother to make wine from these old fashioned ingredients? Surely the answer is that this is where our hobby began and, although the schedules of our larger shows tend to have mostly classes for wines for a special purpose (which I wholeheartedly support), the fact remains that judges are quite often asked to judge at horticultural and other similar small shows where the classification is still on the ingredient basis. Thousands of winemakers throughout the country who are outside the organised movement, are still making, drinking and enjoying real country wines made from the old basic recipes, and jolly good luck to them. If a judge, at some stage of his winemaking career, has not made these wines, how is he going to evaluate their very distinctive qualities? The answer to the problem, excluding the normal balance qualifications, undesirable smells and tastes, must surely be the best of its type that the judge has tasted, unless he has made that wine himself and so be better equipped to evaluate its quality.

A progressive judge will continue to improve his palate recognition and decrease his threshold level for the various components of wine. However, even if we judge wine all our lives, a great number of questions will still be unanswered when we finally hang up our tastevin. As the taste receptors get fatigued by a continual exposure to wine, anything we can do to reduce the length of exposure in the mouth can only be beneficial. This is one good reason why a judge should not spend a long time trying to define off flavours, especially those that are not easily recognised. The palate should be in a good receptive condition for the final evaluation, and not tired and jaded through exposure to bad wines. After all, it is the final selection that the expertise of the judge is of paramount importance.

So much for the judging, but what of the room where the judging takes place? It should be moderate, not hot and not cold, about 65°F (21C). The room should have good window space, preferably facing north, and be free from noises and internal distractions. Artificial lighting, where necessary, should be of the daylight type as some strip lighting will make red wines appear tawny. The room should also be free from alien odours. I once had the misfortune to arrive at a venue and found two massive paraffin heaters with fans going full blast. I can assure you I found the fumes very disconcerting. On another occasion, I had just started tasting when my nose was assailed by a strong acetic acid smell. I sniffed my sample again with some trepidation, thinking I had

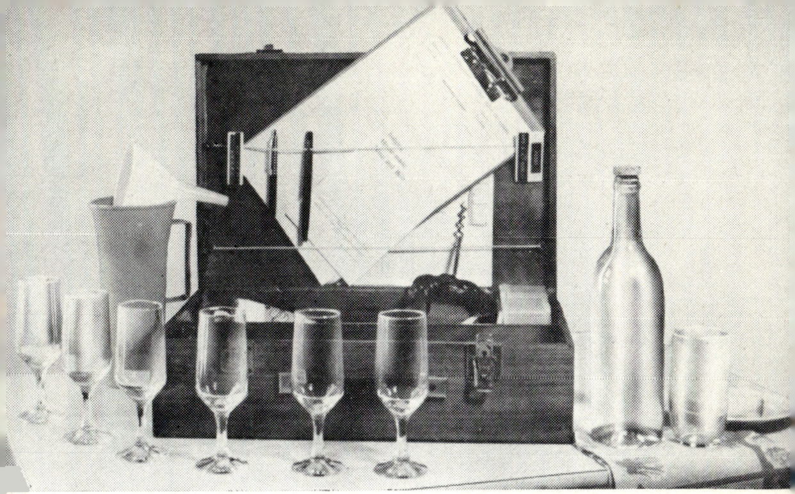

Photo: Charles Torrington

A wine judge's kit. Handbook, marking sheets, pens and pencils, corkscrew, glasscloth, biscuit or cheese-box, six suitable 5 oz. tasting glasses, "spittoon" and funnel, bottle of water and tumbler. And a neat case to carry it all!

Below: Examining for clarity and colour. A.W.N.G.J. judge Don Hebbs at work, watched by his steward Stan Baker.

Photo: Middlesex County Times

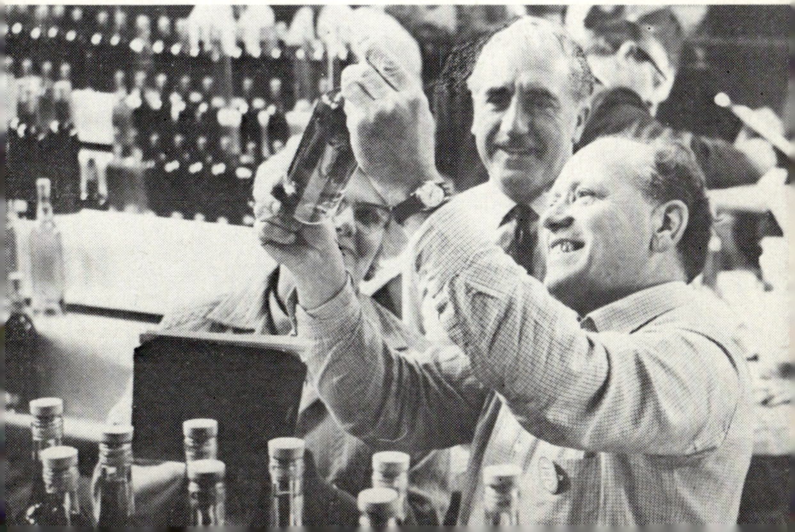

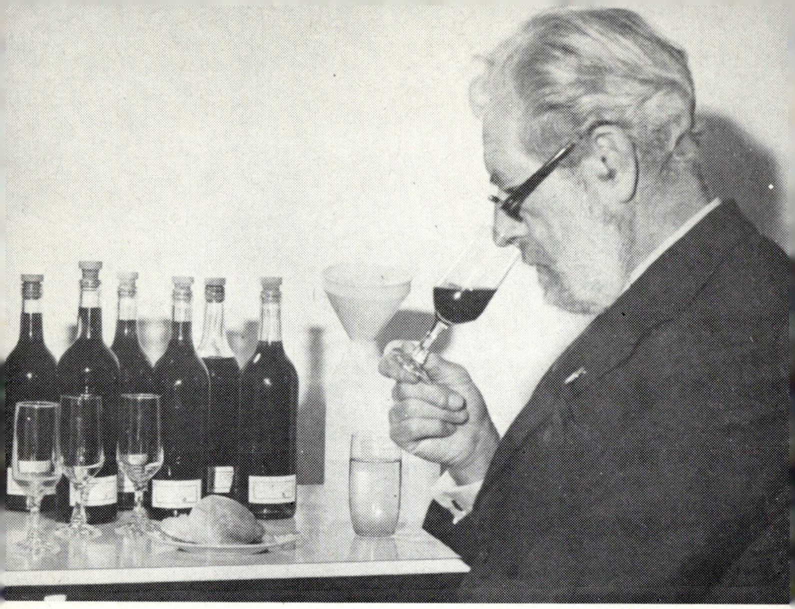

Photo: Charles Torrington

Savouring the bouquet. The author concentrates.

Below: Finalising the short list. A.W.N.G.J. judge H. R. Chandler makes his final selection.

Photo: Charles Torrington

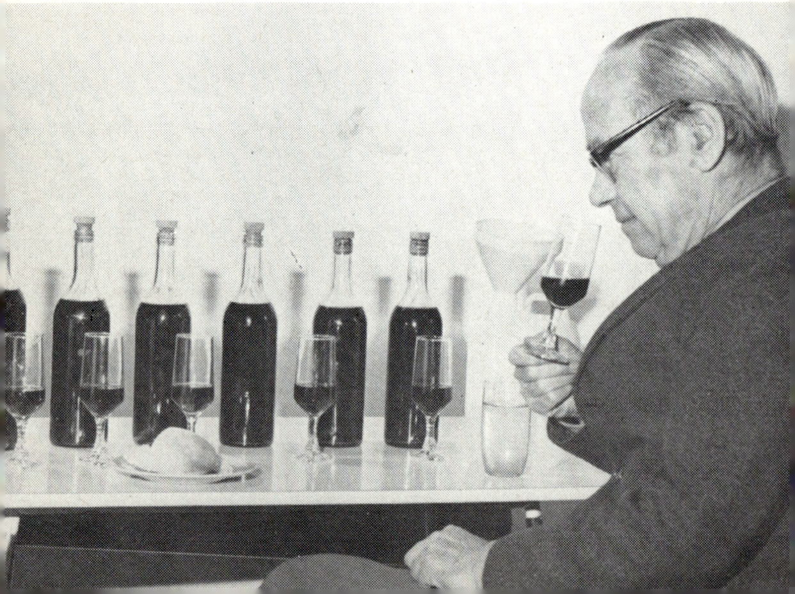

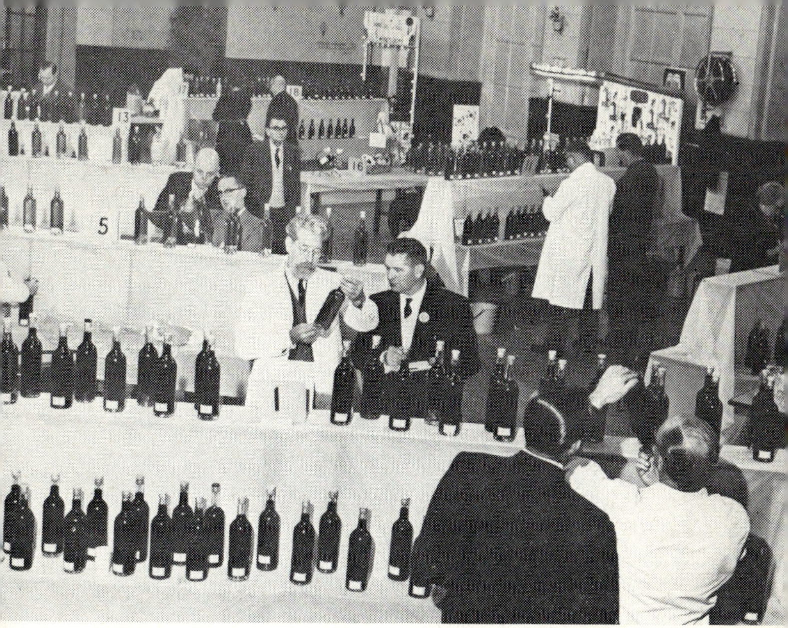

Photo: Middlesex County Times

Judges and their stewards at work at a show.

Below: A beer judge's kit. Some 10 oz. tasting glasses, drying cloth, bread for cleansing palate, bottle opener, "spittoon", water, and candle.

Photo: Charles Torrington

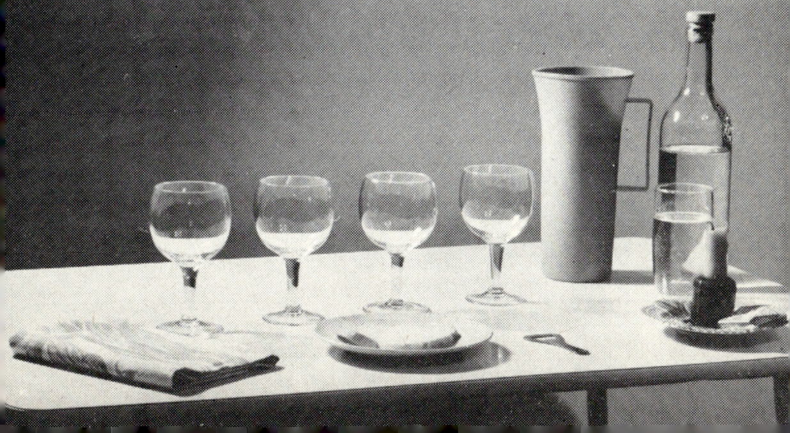

Photo: *Middlesex County Times*

Beer judges at work. Wilf Newsom, A.W.N.G.J., and his steward deep in thought.

missed this on my previous sniff. Finding the sample wholesome, I then looked around for a possible cause. I could see nothing in my immediate surroundings, so I walked down the show bench, the backdrop of which was too high for me to see over, and on the other side—almost opposite to my section —I saw a dear old lady judging the pickle class. (Show organisers please note!)

The wine judge should be comfortable. Whether he sits or stands is a matter for personal preference. I prefer to stand, but I do not consider this point to be very important.

Memory is all-important in wine tasting. Only by comparing the present taste with a previous experience are we able to form an opinion. If one is fond of strawberries, one knows exactly how the first strawberry of the new season will taste—we remember from previous experience. One is continually refreshing and adding to one's memory bank. The more impressions one retains, the sharper the memory and the greater one's efficiency will be. If a judge can recognise an impression quickly, he will take less time in evaluation. This in turn will lengthen the time before the palate becomes fatigued. Memory also plays a very important part when placing the top wines in their final order.

The temperature at which wines are tasted is very important. We prefer, through habit which is based on experience, to drink red table wines at room temperature (although young Beaujolais is now served chilled) and white wine slightly chilled. In a nutshell, slight warmth softens tannins in a wine and a degree of coldness adds crispness to acidity. In practice, we seldom—if ever—find these ideal conditions. At a show, all the different classes are presented at the same temperature. It is, therefore, fairly safe to say a winter show is good for white wines and bad for red and in a summer show, the position is reversed. Of course, a red wine can be slightly warmed by holding the glass in the cupped hands but a white wine, on a hot day, remains a bit flabby.

Finally, the background against which the colour of a wine is being judged is very important. For instance, a red wine judged against a red background will appear lighter in colour, as will a light golden wine judged against a yellow background. Ideally, the backcloth should be neutral, such as off white or light grey.

So much for the background of tasting. Now to the actual technique. . . . It must be systematic, and the following order should always be employed:

White wine before red.
Dry wine before sweet.
Wines with a low alcohol content before those which are high in alcohol.
Heavy dessert and fortified wines to be judged last.

White and red wines should never be mixed, neither should dry and sweet wines. These points should be borne in mind when assessing a composite three-bottle class. The numerical order in which the wines are being tasted is of no importance provided a certain system is followed. Members of The Amateur Winemakers National Guild of Judges follow a standard procedure, starting with the back row of the class and working from left to right.

The first impression obtained of the wine to be

tasted is a visual one. The colour and appearance of the wine in the bottle is observed. This visual examination will reveal faults of clarification or wine spoilage. Bubbles of CO_2 gas indicate that either the wine is still working, has a residual gas content, or is undergoing a malo lactic fermentation. The colour can also indicate defects such as oxidation, lack or excess of fruit. A dirty bottle, or foreign bodies in the wine, would lead the taster to suppose an inferior product.

Having received an overall visual impression, the bottle and its contents are then examined in greater detail. Hold the bottle by placing the thumb in the punt, with the first finger round the base of the bottle and the neck with the other hand. Observe the clarity of the wine and note any haze or suspended material. Look at the bottom to see if any sediment is present. If sediment is not easily discernible, give the bottle a sharp twist with the thumb and forefinger, holding the neck loosely with the other hand. Observe the clarity of the wine and note any haze or suspended material. Look at the bottom to see if any sediment is present. On no account turn the bottle upside down. Notice if any sediment rises from the bottom. Repeat this procedure with all the bottles on the bench.

One advantage of following a set procedure is that the powers of concentration are centred on a limited number of factors. Also, when the actual tasting is being done, the brain can concentrate solely on the reactions on the sensory nerves, without having to break the sequence by further physical examination.

Now return to the first sample. Remove the cork, allow a few moments for the air in the neck to clear, then smell the wine in the bottle. This preliminary smell will enable the taster to recognise a diseased wine and thus prevent contamination of the tasting glass by pouring out a sample.

If the wine is clean, pour a sample into the tasting glass. Take one or two full, quick sniffs, then swirl the glass and again smell the wine. Avoid prolonged weak sniffs as this will hasten adaptation. Concentrate on any off odours that may be present and try to identify them. See if they correspond to any impression remembered from a previous experience. If the wine is clean and healthy, concentrate on any varietal odours, the vinosity and depth of bouquet. Do the smells come off in layers? Is the bouquet strong, light or subtle, or is there a complete lack of bouquet? If the wine is made from fruit and has a strong varietal odour, i.e. smells strongly of a main ingredient, the chances are it will be a fairly young wine. As wine matures, the fruitiness tends to disappear and is replaced by a more mature smell. A strong varietal odour can often mask weaker, volatile smells of a less desirable character. Wines with strong varietal smells should be carefully examined for any underlying smells as such imperfections in the bouquet will only become apparent after some adaptation to the stronger smell has occurred.

Now notice the colour. If a red wine has a purple hue it is probably still quite young. It may also have been made from either black grapes, fresh elderberries or bilberries. If the wine has a very pale colour, it has either been made from fruit with a low colour pigment, has a low fruit content or has insufficient pulp fermentation.

Having examined the bouquet and appearance, the

next step is to take some of the wine into the mouth and evaluate its flavour, balance and texture. If it is a red wine, and it is cold, it is essential to warm it by cupping the glass in the hands for a few moments and retaining the wine in the mouth until it is warm. The wine should be chewed, and swirled around the mouth so that it is in contact with all the taste buds and nerve endings in the various parts of the mouth. A little air is drawn into the mouth through partially opened lips to assist in the release of volatile compounds. Only in this way can an overall impression of the wine be obtained. This is the climax of the evaluation. Everything done so far, from first seeing the bottle, has been building up to this climax. Now is the time for full concentration without distraction. The brains should be fully alert, receiving and analysing messages from the four sets of taste buds, sensory nerve endings of the common chemical sense, the nerves of sense of touch, temperatures and olfactory centre. All this takes place in a fraction of a second! Therefore, I again emphasise that during wine tasting, one should not tolerate any form of distraction. All thoughts should be concentrated on the task in hand.

When the wine is in the mouth, the following points should be noted:

Has the wine any off flavours? Can you recognise them—for instance, a green taste? Is the wine bitter or is there a taste of decomposing vegetation? Is the wine yeasty, can you taste pear drops, acetone, vinegar, excess sulphite, cardboard, disinfectant or iodine? Is the wine pulpy, stemmy, woody, casky, cheesey, musty, mouldy, acrid or medicinal? Is the wine harmonious?

If the wine is supposed to be dry, does it contain too much sugar residue?

If the wine is a red table wine, is the astringency too high or too low? Does it grip the teeth or is it flabby and uninteresting? Has the wine a powerful flavour, or an almost imperceptible one? Is the acidity high, low or correct?

If the wine is a white table wine, is it too acid or does it lack bite? Is it flat and uninteresting or has it too much astringency? Remember, white table wines have a low tannin content compared to red ones. Is the alcohol too high? That goes for both red and white table wines. Is the wine oxidised? Oxidation can be recognised by colour, bouquet and taste, so there are three ways of detecting this fault, but only bouquet and taste will confirm it. Has the wine been left too long in a cask, as this will give it a woody or casky taste?

In the case of a dessert wine, has it the right amount of wine extract or body, with the right sugar residue? Is it smooth or coarse on the palate? Is it full flavoured with a high alcohol content, is the impression harmonious?

If the wine is in a "by ingredient" class, is the flavour distinct i.e. apple, elderflower, citrus etc., or have other ingredients with a predominant flavour been added?

Draw a little air into the mouth through the lips, this will help to release volatile compounds, then exhale through the nose over the olfactory nerves and the smell sensations will combine with those of taste to give an overall impression.

Having evaluated the wine, eject it into a spittoon. A few drops will be retained in the mouth and when swallowed, one is left with the sensation of wine in the mouth. This is commonly spoken of as "the farewell of the wine" and is an important aspect of wine tasting. Concentrate on the "feel" in the mouth. Does the mouth feel clean and fresh? Can you still taste the flavour of the wine, and is the sensation one that gives you pleasure or does your mouth feel hot, rough or unpleasant, or is there very little of anything? A good wine will leave nothing but favourable impressions, and this is called "a pleasant farewell". Some wines, although quite pleasant when in the mouth, leave very little impression once the wine has been ejected. Such wines lack life and have little character. The farewell can be unclean or with unpleasant flavours lingering in the mouth for a long time after the wine has been ejected, hence the importance of a palate cleanser. A very common fault amongst home-made wines is a bitter farewell. This may be due to excessive tannins, wild yeast, insufficient acid in the must, or carelessness in the preparation of the basic ingredients such as the inclusion of the pith in citrus fruits.

Chapter 9
Judging Procedure

When judging a class of wine, it is essential the procedure be organised and systematic, otherwise there is great danger of mistakes occurring which would be embarrassing to both the judge and the show secretary. It should be remembered that the exhibitors have spent a lot of time, patience and energy in the making and preparation of their exhibits. You can imagine the disappointment and annoyance of an exhibitor who finds, for instance, that his exhibit has not been judged or has inadvertently been staged in the wrong class by a well meaning steward who, perhaps, was working under pressure. Many people forget that everyone who is involved in the organising and staging of a winemaking show, is himself an amateur and is giving freely of his time and energy without any form of payment, except the knowledge that he has done a good job of work for his hobby.

The judge should also remember that he has been honoured by being asked to judge others' efforts. He can, of course, if qualified by examination, be justifiably proud of his recognised standing in the hobby, and providing he tempers his pride with humility to his fellow winemakers, no harm can come of that. On the other hand, any judge who is dogmatic or arrogant will soon find himself without work; invitations to judge just will not be forth-coming!

The primary object of a judge is to find the best exhibits in his class, and then to place those exhibits in order of merit. By using his knowledge and expertise, he can also tell the exhibitor what is wrong with his wine and, within the limits of his knowledge, advise how best to avoid or rectify the faults. This will not be possible unless he adopts a systematic approach to his procedure at the show bench.

The judge will be invited to attend the briefing of the judges and stewards. This duty is usually per-formed by the convenor of judges or the show secretary.

At the briefing, the judge will be allocated the class he is to judge. He will also be allocated a steward, who will assist him. The Convenor will acquaint the judge with any local rules or directions appertaining to that particular show. The judge will most probably be given an envelope containing the marking sheet, a result sheet, award cards, placing stickers for the winning bottles of wine and a badge for himself and his steward. Where lunch is provided there may also be tickets for that.

Following the briefing, the judge, accompanied by his steward, will go to his class in the judging room. On arrival, he will set out his judging equipment on the table provided by the organisers, ask his steward to obtain water for rinsing the tasting glasses and, where required, water for palate cleansing. At this point, the judge should inspect his hands and if practicable, wash them and rinse them well. When judging wine, the hands should be free from external odour and this, of course, includes scented soap. The judge may have travelled a long distance by car, arriving just in time for the briefing and it is always possible that his hands are travel stained.

Now, affix the marking sheet to the marking board and make sure that your steward is aware of the judging procedure. If he is not, instruct him accordingly and commence work. Enter on your marking sheet, under the appropriate heading, your name, the name of the venue and the date. Make sure that the class number of your section corresponds to that on your briefing envelope.

If you have been told how many bottles you are to judge, count them and make sure that you have the correct number. One missing can spell trouble at an "inquest" after the show.

Glance along the rows of bottles and observe the colour of the exhibits. I have, on several occasions, found a white wine in a red class and a red wine in a white class—the exhibits had inadvertently been staged in the wrong class. Should this happen, ask your steward to take the exhibit to the right class.

Check the class numbers on all your exhibits. Again, you may find an exhibit in the wrong class. Stewards are human, and in common with us all, liable to error. If a mistake has been made, it is better to rectify it at this early stage so as not to inconvenience the judge of the class involved.

The time has now arrived to tackle the physical appraisal of the exhibits. To save time, and to facilitate easy working, hand your marking sheet to your steward and instruct him to write down the exhibitor's number and the points you award under the appropriate heading. Always check that no errors have been made.

Remove the bottle on the extreme left of the back row and note the exhibitor's number. Examine the bottle for presentation (two marks). Note that the shape and colour of the bottle is according to schedule. If in doubt, consult the Convenor of Judges and let him give a ruling. Note that the cork is the right type and that the bottle is labelled according to instructions. At some of the shows the labelling instructions are sent out with the labels and are not included in the show schedules. Where this happens, ask your steward to obtain a copy from the show secretary. An exhibit is only disqualified if it is not according to schedule (N.A.S.); any other fault will result in downpointing. Examine the bottle and cork for cleanliness. If the bottle is dirty or has gum smears from the label, deduct one point. If the cork is obviously dirty, deduct one point. Provided the cork is clean it should not lose points for being of poor quality as it is extremely difficult in some parts of the country to obtain corks that are of top quality. Scratches on the bottle do not lose points, but if the bottle is chipped, it will be downpointed. Handling smears on a well polished bottle may have been caused by handling at the show, so in this case the exhibitor is given the benefit of the doubt.

Having awarded the points for presentation, examine the wine for clarity. The National standard is to award from nought to four points. The wine to gain the highest points must be starbright or of brilliant appearance and the wine should scintillate from the punt. In the past, it was a rare occurrence to find many starbright wines but with the advent of more sophisticated filter aids, more polished wines are now appearing.

The next stage down is the well cleared wine. This is the condition of most of the exhibits. The wine is completely free from haze, sediment and floaters, but not polished.

After the clear wines come those with haze, sediment, floaters or a combination of any of the three. Another fault frequently met is inhomogeneity. This is a wine, perhaps, to which sugar syrup has been added which has not thoroughly blended with the wine. The syrup lies in a dense layer on the bottom of the bottle. Wines are deducted points according to the amount of solid matter present. For instance, a milky wine with sediment will score no points for clarity. This condition usually indicates a very young wine which has not thrown out its yeast cells. A wine that has a moderate haze and no sediment or a slight sediment but no haze, will score one point. For a very slight haze or a wisp of sediment when the bottle is rotated (see chapter on judging technique), two points can be awarded. For inhomogeneity, points are deducted according to the degree of the fault. Isolated, suspended, solid particles or particles lying on the bottom of the bottle will result in the deduction of one to three points according to the quantity.

The bottle is now replaced in its original position on the show bench and the same procedure is adopted for the remainder of the class, each row being examined from left to right. The colour of the wine, which should be in accordance with the class, is considered with the clarity. Instability of the wine may also be noticed during this physical appraisal. It is unnecessary to spend a long time searching for the faults, because if present, they will be readily seen.

Now take the marking sheet from your steward and ask him to give you the first exhibit from the show bench. To avoid error, the number of the exhibit is checked with the first number on your marking sheet. This procedure is repeated each time a fresh bottle is brought forward. Ask your steward to remove the cork from the bottle, allow a few moments for the stale air to clear from the bottle and then smell the wine. Should it smell of acetic acid, replace the cork and return the bottle to the show bench. Such a wine will receive no marks for bouquet and taste. Enter "Acetified" in the remarks column of your marking sheet.

If the wine is not acetified, proceed with its evaluation. The initial smell will tell the experienced judge many things. The wine may have, for instance, a strong fruity smell or may be varietal, such as raspberry or elderflower. There may be off odours which can be easily recognised such as greenness or oxidation. There can, of course, be an almost complete lack of smell, indicating a poorly made wine or one that has not been well cellared. This appraisal is only a preliminary to the evaluation in the glass. Ideally, from a judge's point of view, any wine with definite off odours should be returned to the show bench. However, as the exhibitor will expect some helpful advice later on, it is necessary to give the wine further appraisal. It is left to the judge how far he is prepared to go in this direction. In any case, an off smell at this stage MAY just come from the stale air in the neck of the bottle.

Now instruct the steward to pour a sample into a

tasting glass. The sample should be sufficient but not wasteful, as any wine which remains in the glass after the tasting is discarded into the spittoon and should not be poured back into the bottle or used in any other way. About half an ounce is sufficient for one taste—it can be repeated if necessary. Notice if the wine is stable. If you can see bubbles of CO_2 rising in the glass as the wine is poured, the wine is down-pointed according to the amount of instability. If it is very bubbly, the wine will not be further evaluated. On the other hand, it may only have a very slight gas residue which will clear when the wine is poured.

Generally speaking, any gassy wine will affect the common chemical sense when taken into the mouth, it will give a prickly sensation on the tongue and mouth tissues. Although a slight degree of petillance is acceptable in some commercial table wines, and in some cases enhances the wine, at this moment it is considered a fault in exhibition wine.

Hold the glass by the foot and take a quick sniff, then swirl the wine in the glass and take one or two quick sniffs. Remove the glass from your nose and continue to concentrate on what you have smelled.

A good red wine should have depth, be full and harmonious. Some white table wines have fragrant, subtle bouquets—the bouquet should at all times be compatible with the type of wine. It should have vinosity, a fruity smell, which need not be strong according to its class, and be completely free from any undesirable odours.

If the class is varietal, the bouquet should be characteristic of the base ingredient and not over-powered or distorted by additional ingredients.

If the wine is very mature the original varietal

smell may have disappeared, but it is unlikely that a wine on the show bench will be that old!

If the wine has off odours, try to distinguish them according to the definitions enumerated under "Savouring the bouquet". Award marks according to the quality of the bouquet from one to four. A wine with serious off odours will receive no marks for bouquet.

Write your comments in the remarks column. They should be brief and descriptive, such as green, oxidised, fruity, subtle, musty etc. If abbreviations are used, the judge should be able to recognise them later. The bouquet of a wine should always be in keeping with its class. For example, a table wine should have a light pleasing bouquet. It may be slightly fruity but not too powerful, vinous but not too alcoholic. A dessert wine, on the other hand, can carry a much fuller and more fruity bouquet with a high vinosity. Varietal wines should be descriptive of their type but not overpowering. There is nothing worse than an overpowering elderflower wine where too many petals have been used.

I am reminded of the inadvisability of having too much wine in the tasting glass by an episode at a show where the judge remarked to his steward, "this wine has a clinging bouquet". "I am not surprised, Sir", replied the steward. "You have a drop of it on the end of your nose"!

Having evaluated the bouquet, the judge now comes to that part of the procedure where it is essential to direct all his powers of concentration to the job in hand. It is the time for tasting. This can be one of his most enjoyable experiences—or one of his worst, it all depends on the wine! Take a small amount of the wine into the mouth, sufficient to cover the whole surface of the tongue. The wine is chewed and where necessary, warmed in the mouth, as in the case of a cold red wine. A little air is drawn into the mouth and the volatilised odours exhaled. Notice if the wine has any undesirable tastes; if so, can you recognise them? How severe is the off flavour, slight, mild or very bad? If the latter, it may be very difficult to judge the wine for balance. In any case, one does not retain a bad wine in the mouth long enough to find out, but in the few seconds the wine is in contact with the palate, you may have noticed excessive acid or tannin. Deduct marks for any imperfection of flavour. If the off flavour is only very slight or if the wine is clean, concentrate on any imperfections of balance such as high or low total acidity, alcohol content, tannin, body, sugar residue and flavour. At the same time, notice whether the wine is harmonious, does the overall impression give pleasure, have all the components married successfully, or does the wine have rough edges? Any imperfections in balance will result in a loss of marks, and the number of marks deducted will depend on the degree of imbalance.

Up to 20 marks are awarded for balance, flavour and overall impression. The reader may wonder how to arrive at a decision, and how many marks to award or deduct. This can be done in two ways. One way is to give an overall score without any numerical points on balance, flavour etc. This system can only be applied successfully by an experienced judge because his decisions are made by comparing the wine under test to previous experiences with a similar type of wine. He also will have a low threshold level for the various components of the wine which, in turn, will enable him to make his decision more quickly. The alternative way is to award marks for each component of balance. The following scale may be useful for a lesser experienced or an aspirant judge:

BALANCE

Component	Top rating perfect balance	Good rating good balance	Medium rating slight im-balance	Low rating poor balance
Total Acid	3	$2\frac{1}{2}$	2	1
Alcohol content	3	$2\frac{1}{2}$	2	1
Tannin	3	$2\frac{1}{2}$	2	1
Sugar residue	3	$2\frac{1}{2}$	2	1
Flavour	3	$2\frac{1}{2}$	2	1
Body	2	$1\frac{1}{2}$	1	$\frac{1}{2}$
Texture, roughness, smoothness etc.	3	2	1	$\frac{1}{2}$
Total	20	16	12	6

Very few wines will be perfect. The majority will be in the middle categories. It should be remembered that some components may be influencing others. For instance, alcohol has a moderating effect on acid, so that in certain types of wine, two wines with different amounts of acidity may score equal marks. On the other hand, a wine with a low alcohol content may lose marks against a wine with a higher alcohol content, but with an equal amount of total acid. Acid has a modifying effect on sugar and sugar lessens the effect of tannin. An example of using the numerical system is as follows:

A dry table wine with the correct sugar residue would score 3 points, correct acidity 3 points, slightly over-astringent 2 points, low body $\frac{1}{2}$ point, excess alcohol 1 point, good flavour $2\frac{1}{2}$ points, rough impression on the after palate 1 point, giving a total of 13 points, which would give the wine an average to good rating depending on the overall standard of the class.

A suggestion for marking using the overall score system is:

Perfect 20 points. Very good 16–18 points. Good 14–16 points. Average 10–14 points. Poor 6–10 points and for a bad wine, no points. The effect of the wine on the after palate is considered and marked under the overall impression.

After sampling the wine, eject it into the spittoon, award marks according to the quality and make your comments in the remarks column. Remarks for the quoted example would read "Fairly well balanced, clean but a little too astringent, alcohol too high for a table wine, lacking in body with a rough finish; would probably improve with keeping".

The first wine to be tasted is usually taken as a yardstick for those which follow. If it is an average wine, with no serious faults in the bouquet and flavour but no balance, it would be a good plan to mark it about halfway in the overall palate appraisal, that is award it 10–11 marks. This will leave plenty of room for manoeuvre upwards for a wine of better quality or downwards for the poorer wines. It is a mistake to mark a wine too high unless it is a first class wine when, of course, it should be marked accordingly. By the same token a faulty wine would receive less than the suggested marks. If you disqualify a wine, note the reason on the marking sheet and affix the necessary label to the bottle.

NOW CLEANSE YOUR PALATE.

Ask your steward to return the exhibit to its original place on the show bench and bring the next one forward. The reason for having only one bottle on the tasting table is to make absolutely sure that no error occurs by mixing up the exhibits. Some judges prefer to use the small batch system, that is, having several bottles on the tasting table at the same time, but this procedure is not recommended for inexperienced judges. I always follow the procedure as recommended by the A.W.N.G.J.

After you have smelled the wine in the second bottle, ask your steward to pour a sample into a clean glass, then rinse your first tasting glass and stand it to drain. Now repeat the procedure as for the first exhibit. This procedure is then followed for remainder of the class.

A careful judge will always note the number of the exhibit against the number on the marking sheet; even the most competent steward is not infallible—like the judge he may have an off day!

When you have judged seven or eight wines, go back to the first wine and re-taste it—you will then have a comparison, It is a good plan to re-taste some of your earlier selections, particularly when the class is a large one. This reassessment is a very useful way of checking your palate reaction. This is most relevant when judging a class of heavy dessert wines with high alcohol and sugar residue. Sugar reduces the tartness in an acid wine and if the class of dessert wines is a large one, palate adaptation to sugar may occur as the tasting proceeds, and an early selection that appeared well balanced may now have a slight acid taste.

The marks allocated to a wine at the initial appraisal are not necessarily the final indication of its quality as this can only be established during the final assessment. For example, a wine that is marked at 15 for overall impression may be placed higher than a wine that was marked at 16. Some wines with very bad faults may not receive any marks at all for overall impression. When faced with a class of 50 or more wines to judge, trying to assess correctly the relative position of a bad wine is of no merit. It is of far greater importance to place the wines of near equal quality in the correct order. At the same time, a faulty wine is assessed and remarks made in the appropriate place. This will be useful to both judge and competitor during the question session. There are, of course, occasions when each wine, good or bad, has to be carefully marked. For instance, there will be times when one is asked to evaluate a given number of wines against one or two sets of similar wines. This is a different matter and will be dealt with later in this book.

Having assessed each exhibit in the class, the next step is to total the marks and select those wines with the highest points. This selection may be anywhere between four and eight bottles, depending on the quality of the class. If there are several wines with equal marks at the lower end of the selection, these can be reassessed and the best brought forward.

Chapter 10
Finalising the Short List

We now come to the most critical part of the palate assessment. Up to this point, the judge has been eliminating wines with faults and selecting wines of quality, but he now has to assess the finer points of the quality wines and in some cases, these can be very marginal.

This is where his palate and experience are exercised to the full. Memory is of vital importance as he must remember all the aspects of each wine during this assessment.

Let us assume that we have six exhibits on the short list which are marked 18, 17, 17, 16, 15½ and 15. The marks would indicate very little difference between the first three placings, but the quality was falling off at the tail end of the selection. This, in itself, is an important psychological point. The judge has probably already formed an opinion that wines 1, 2 and 3 are of superior quality. This is probably quite correct but nevertheless, the short list has to be reassessed and any step which will help the judge to give an unbiased opinion when deciding the awards must be taken.

As blind tasting is impractical, and in any case undesirable as it restricts one's sensory evaluation, another method must, therefore, be adopted to prevent the judge recognising the exhibits. The steward is instructed to withdraw the selection from the show bench using the list of exhibitors numbers given to him by the judge. The judge will check the numbers to make sure there is no error. The steward is then instructed to mix up the exhibits, place them in a single row on the tasting table with the labels away from the judge, and to place a clean tasting glass in front of each bottle.

Whilst this is being done, and time permitting, the judge should leave the show bench and go for a short stroll. If the weather is fine, a 5 or 10 minute stroll in the open air will help to relax him and prepare him for the task in hand. In any case, the judge should leave the show bench whilst the bottles are being set up.

On his return, the judge should check that the tasting glasses are in place, his drinking water container for palate cleaning is full and his spittoon is strategically placed. Everything is done with a view to avoid distraction whilst the final evaluation takes place. This is the time when the thoughts of the judge must be concentrated wholly on the task in hand.

The judge has now to evaluate the finer points of quality. Each wine is reassessed according to its merits and the qualities of each wine have to be remembered right through the selection. The steward is instructed not to talk during this evaluation and to prevent any outside interference. The steward is now instructed to pour about two ounces of wine from each bottle into its respective glass. The judge should then cleanse his palate and proceed with the tasting. Where one or two wines are very close in quality, it may be necessary to taste the wines more than once before deciding on their placing. When the final placings have been made, the exhibits are placed in order of merit i.e. 1, 2, 3, 4 etc. The wines are now given a final tasting but starting at the bottom of the selection and working to the top. This experience should be like climbing a ladder—the palate sensation should be a continual ascending one.

The colour of the wine is carefully considered during this assessment. It may be that two wines are equally assessed on overall impression. In this case, the colour of the wine may be the deciding factor in its placings. In practice, this very seldom happens.

Having decided on the placing, ask your steward to wash your glasses and empty your spittoon and glass rinsing water. Now affix the bottle stickers, 1st, 2nd etc., to the winning exhibits if these are supplied. Fill in your result sheet and take it to the show convenor where requested, otherwise ask your steward to do so. Make sure that your section of the show bench is left in a clean and orderly condition—nothing looks worse than an untidy show bench. Remember that the public will be viewing the classes after the opening of the show. Your last chore will be to complete your Judges Comment Sheet or Judges Report, where provided. These reports are usually staged for perusal by the exhibitors and general public.

A word about the comments in this report. Be brief, lucid, use meaningful definitions and, where possible, be helpful. Nothing is gained by unkind criticism. If a class has a very low standard, try to assess any common faults and then mention them. Where possible, give the cause and suggest a remedy or how to avoid them. If a number of wines are harsh and astringent, being probably young, and would improve with good cellaring—say so.

By trying to be helpful, you will gain the confidence and respect of the exhibitors—adverse criticism helps no one, It may even deter and dishearten some of the inexperienced exhibitors but on the other hand, constructive criticism can only do good. Good liaison between judge and competitor is one sure way of improving wine quality.

A class that invokes a certain amount of discussion from the judging point of view is the three-bottle class. This class usually comprises one bottle of red dry table wine, one bottle of white table wine dry and one bottle of red or white dessert wine. Here we have three bottles of different wine, but as one entry, and therefore, have to be considered as a whole. The task of evaluating may be approached in two ways.

1. Either you judge each type separately, i.e. the white dry followed by the red dry, followed by the dessert, or

2. Judge all the white dry wines, followed by the red dry wines, and last of all the dessert wines.

What are the relative merits of each method? The unit evaluation gives an immediate idea of the overall quality of the entry, whereas the single type method, particularly if the class is a large one, will not have this advantage as it will be extremely difficult to remember in detail the smaller characteristics of each wine. On the other hand, the unit method will be very hard on the palate as the red dry wine would be wedged between the white table and the dessert wine. The red table wine following the white table wine would be a possibility, but the heavy dessert wine following the astringent red table wine is far from ideal, and finally the white table wine, with its delicate intricacies following the sweet dessert wine will be somewhat disconcerting.

If the single wine system is followed, there is no real problem from the palate point of view, as normal judging procedure is observed. My choice on balance is for the single type method, modified to include the unit appraisal where necessary for finalising the short list. The marking system for the single type method has to vary slightly from normal procedure inasmuch as three lines must be left for each entry. For example:

Exhibit No. 21

White wine	Total marks 17
Red wine	,, ,, 14
Dessert wine	,, ,, 16

TOTAL 47

Exhibit No. 22

White wine	Total marks 14
Red wine	,, ,, 17
Dessert wine	,, ,, 15

TOTAL 46

And so on. In a three bottle class, one often finds two good wines and one bad, this does not present any real difficulty as the discrepancy in quality is reflected on the total marks.

It sometimes happens that one or more classes in a show have too many exhibits to be dealt with competently by one judge, and two judges may be allocated to the class. The two judges each take one half of the class. They judge their half of the class independently and select their short list. The stewards are then instructed to mix the selected bottles and stage them in line with the labels away from the judges. The judges then reassess all the selection and award points for each exhibit. After the assessment, they arrange their marks in the following manner. Let us suppose there were seven bottles in the final selection.

Exhibit	1	2	3	4	5	6	7
Judge No. 1	17	15	18	14	17	18	16
Judge No. 2	18	16	18	15	15	16	17
TOTAL	35	31	36	29	32	34	33

The result would be first No. 3, second No. 1, third No. 6 etc. In the event of a tie, the two judges reassess the two wines and come to an agreement. Two experienced judges working together harmoniously will come to an agreement on the selection purely by palate assessment. I have shared in this experience on a number of occasions and have never experienced any difficulty, in fact both my co-judge and I have found the experience both rewarding and enjoyable.

Another method is to have a third judge to finalise the two short lists. This system is not always popular as some judges prefer to place their own selections. This, of course, is understandable as there is a feeling of having done only half the job and the ultimate satisfaction of placing the wines of quality is the most rewarding part of the assessment. Nevertheless, there is some merit in having a third judge as his palate will be completely fresh and untired.

A query which sometimes arises when deciding on trophy winners, and I refer now to "The Best Wine In Show", is whether to include the three bottle class for this award. If one is impartial and correct, I would suggest that the best bottle from the three bottle class should be included. This may mean that the best bottle of wine is not amongst the prize winners in that class as it often happens that a really first class wine is accompanied by two bad ones. Nevertheless, that bottle of wine is entered correctly as an exhibit in the show and I think it should receive consideration.

My personal opinion is that the award "Best in Show" should be replaced by the exhibitor gaining the highest aggregate points in the classes, thereby rewarding the consistent maker of quality wines.

FORTIFIED WINES

When judging a fortified wine class, the judge must be conversant with the wine that is being evaluated i.e. sherry type, or port type, otherwise what are his standards? A judge who has only an occasional drink of dry sherry and then insists on one particular brand, is in no way equipped to evaluate a dry sherry type wine; the same applies to port type wine. The obvious answer is for the judge to gain as much experience as he can by drinking sherry of all types and port wine at every available opportunity, also to vary the brands so that he acquires the necessary knowledge that will enable him to give a good appraisal. I can state from experience that this exercise does not inflict any hardship! What is mportant is to fix the characteristics in one's memory bank and in this way gain knowledge on which to make one's assessment. A judge who is not conversant with fortified wines should decline to judge such a class.

APERITIFS

The aperitif class is another class which presents certain difficulties for a judge. How, for instance, does one assess a vermouth type wine against a Campari type, or a Martini type? The exercise is fraught with danger. A heavily bittered vermouth may be followed by a light delicate orange wine with a modicum of pith bitterness which, by itself, could be a very nice aperitif, but its subtle quality could be swamped by a badly made vermouth to which too much essence had been added. The same would apply to a nice crisp dry sherry type wine. If, however, the aperitifs were labelled by type, the judge could select each type and judge them separately, then bring forward the best of each section for final appraisal. This would ease the situation and be less demanding on the palate but in any case, the judge will have to work very hard at keeping his palate in condition for the final assessment. Surely, the answer is to have an aperitif class of one type, only then will the class become manageable. Ultimately, I feel there will always be some palate preference in classes of this nature. I think the amateur winemaking fraternity is expecting rather a lot of a judge of WINE to give an accurate assessment of all these classes.

LIQUEURS

The above comments apply equally to a class of liqueurs. I know that these classes are very popular at some of the wine shows and far be it from me to decry their inclusion. At the same time, as this book is intended to be helpful from the judging point of view, it would be wrong of me to dismiss the subject without putting forward any views purely as a judge.

The first thing to consider is how to judge a large class of liqueurs and finish up sober! Liqueurs are usually fairly high in alcohol—I have been offered some which took my breath away. They taste very well with coffee after a dinner, but the thought of judging 20 or 30 of them in cold blood at 10 a.m., particularly when they include creme de menthe, "Benedictine", coffee, "Advokaat", cherry, "Drambuie" etc., is not exactly enticing. I cannot help feeling that the palate of a judge is not intended for this kind of exercise.

Nevertheless, so long as these classes are included in the show schedules, someone will be invited to judge them. So what can be done to minimise the difficulties from the judge's point of view? One thing seems fairly obvious. First limit the alcohol content— the spirit content should be compatible with the liqueur being emulated. The next obvious point is to have a liqueur class of all the same type, i.e. cherry brandy type, Benedictine type etc. This would, of course, probably result in a reduced entry. Whilst I am not suggesting that any exhibitor would resort to a little skilfull "blending", this fact has to be faced, and it would be very difficult to prove.

Another alternative is to stipulate that the liqueur must have been made by fruit infusion i.e. plum brandy, peach brandy etc., then the task of the judge would be greatly simplified. What is more, the product would be truly "home made" which in turn, wouid require expertise on the part of the maker. In this case, entries would have a marked similarity. So long as the mixed liqueur class exists, I would suggest that the judge divides the entries into brandy and clear spirit sections, then sub-divide the entries into types and judge each type separately, retaining the sample in the mouth only long enough to make a decision, then eating a piece of dry bread and rinsing the mouth well with water between each sample. With the high sugar residue of the liqueurs there is a very real danger of sugar adaptation occuring.

Where the liqueurs have been made by the simple method of mixing sugar syrup, essences and alcohol together, the question of balance, and I speak now in terms of wine balance, does not occur, but where they have been made by infusing fruit in alcohol, a question of balance will arise e.g. plum brandy. In such cases the acidity and astringency, if present, must be in balance with the remainder of the ingredients. The overall impression should be one of the right degree of sweetness compatible with the alcohol content and flavour, and the finished product should be smooth and devoid of harshness. The flavour should not be too strong of its type, but strong enough to give a pleasant impression of the ingredients.

MEAD

Mead or honey wine is also in a class of its own. A judge, in order to assess mead, should have made considerable amounts of mead over the years and have had experience in drinking not only his own mead, but mead made by others. It is a great advantage if the judge is an apiarist of some years standing, as this experience will provide the background to his knowledge of honey which is essential to successful meadmaking when using English honey, and this in turn will help him to judge mead. As the many flavours of commercial wine are greatly influenced by the variety of grapes used in its production, so are the flavours of mead influenced by the different honeys.

A palatable mead, suitable for use as a table wine, is made by using a light coloured honey such as clover as this will give the mead a light bouquet and a mild flavour. A dry mead made from a dark honey, such as heather honey, would be most unpalatable because of its strong flavour but the same honey would make a very pleasant heavy dessert mead. The higher sugar and alcohol content would bring the flavour into balance. As a general rule, one could say light honey for a dry mead, medium to dark honey for a sweet mead, and dark honey for a dessert mead. One can also make a heavy dessert mead from medium honey. For Pyment, made from pure fresh grape juice and honey, a light honey is used. This also applies to Hippocras, which is made from grape juice, honey and spices. For a dry metheglin, made from honey, water and spices, again a light honey is used but for a sweet metheglin, a honey of medium colour is used. Cyser, made from apple juice and honey, should be made with light honey. Melomels, made from fruit juice sweetened with honey, are better made with a light honey. If a strongly flavoured honey is used, there is a danger of the fruit and honey flavours clashing, resulting in some very queer and unpalatable off flavours. A medicinal flavour in mead is usually caused by insufficient acid in the must.

The National Honey Show Schedule stipulates that for general dry and sweet mead classes, the mead should be made from honey and water through the process of fermentation, but the use of yeast nutrient and acid to give the mead balance is accepted.

Mead has a flavour of its own and not everyone likes it. Some honey gives mead a "smokey" flavour which is quite pleasant—I use the term smokey for want of a better description. Basically, mead is judged for its balance, as is wine. The main difference lies in its flavour and the flavour has to be in keeping with its type. The same procedure is adopted for a mead class as for a class of wine.

Some schedules have a mixed class of metheglin and melomels. In this case, the judge separates the two types and judges the melomels first, as metheglin contains spices. The metheglin section is then judged and, for the final assessment, the best of each section is selected. Again, the melomels receive the first assessment. This mixed class is not easy to judge and it would be better to have two separate classes.

Chapter 11
The Role of the Steward

The person allocated to you as a steward is there either because he volunteered to help the judge as part of his work towards the overall success of the show, and therefore has very little interest in the actual judging procedure, or because he has volunteered in order to learn the art of judging wine, and to further his knowledge on the subject. Most of the stewards belong to the latter category, but I have had a few stewards who stated quite plainly that they were not really interested in judging and had no desire to taste the wines.

All stewards are volunteers, and the judge's approach to his steward should be friendly and tactful. It is important to establish friendly contact with your steward at once. Some stewards are quite nervous, particularly if they are stewarding for a well known judge so, if necessary, put your steward at ease by talking to him whilst you are preparing your equipment. You can, of course, have a steward who is so talkative that you cannot get a word in edge-wise! Ascertain that your steward is conversant with his duties. If not, explain to him what is required and what your procedure, from start to finish, will be. This will obviate breaking your concentration during judging. If your steward is there solely to do a job of work, you can concentrate on your judging but at the same time, check that he is not making any errors, such as bringing the wrong bottle forward. If, on the other hand, your steward expresses a desire to learn, then this is quite another matter.

Ask him questions about his background in winemaking before you start judging. Does he wish to take the Guild examination ultimately? What is his experience? Has he won prizes? How many times has he stewarded, and for whom? His answers will give you a good idea of his ability.

If your steward wishes to sample wine with you, ask him to provide himself with a couple of tasting glasses. Impress upon your steward that any remarks you may make about the exhibits are for his ears alone and should not be repeated—remarks given in confidence MUST NEVER BE REPEATED.

So much for the general approach to stewarding, now for the way of judging. First of all, show your steward what you are looking for when you examine the first exhibit for presentation, clarity and colour. Explain how you award points; do it quietly but in detail. There is nothing more annoying to other judges working on either side of you than a judge who is talking in loud tones to his steward.

Having explained your procedure with the first exhibit, carry on with the appraisal of the remaining exhibits but draw his attention to any point which you think might be constructive, such as inhomogeneity.

When it comes to the tasting, ask him to pour two samples—one for you and one for himself. Sample your wine, award your marks, write down your comments and then ask your steward for his opinion.

THEN, you can briefly discuss the wine with him. If there is anything exceptional about the wine and he missed it, ask him to have a second taste to see if he can identify it. Ask his opinion on the acidity and, where applicable, the astringency, the sugar and alcohol content of the wine. If there is an off odour or flavour in the sample, see if he can identify it. The amount of time you devote to this kind of exercise will obviously depend on the size of the class you have to judge and the amount of time you have to complete the judging. If you repeat the comparative tasting process with your steward for the first eight or nine wines, you may be able to form an opinion as to the steward's palate for balance. He may, for instance, remark that all wines are low in acid when, in fact, the acid balance may be correct in most cases. This may indicate a high threshold for acidity on his part —he may be used to drinking very acid wines. Draw his attention to this and advise accordingly.

One golden rule, never allow your steward to make comments about a wine unless he has been asked to do so.

There is, of course, no merit in telling your steward your opinion before asking for his. The chances are that he would agree with you, although he thought differently before. His opinion would probably be influenced by your remarks.

Proceed with the comparative tasting but keep a careful watch on the time. You may find that there is insufficient time to repeat this exercise for the whole of the class and in this case, limit your comparative tasting to any samples which you think may have some exceptional smell or taste which would be instructive to your steward. Limit your conversation to the evaluation of the wines being sampled and to explaining the various points that arise. It is a mistake to give a mini-lecture on winemaking as your steward will be only able to assimilate a certain amount of knowledge, therefore stick to the essentials.

Diversions can also break the concentration of a judge and that must, at all times, be devoted to the task on hand. Should your steward accidentally break one of your tasting glasses, adopt an attitude of casual indifference as he will be feeling very remorseful, so put him at ease. I once had three glasses out of six broken during one judging session and had to borrow glasses to finalise my short list. I must confess, my sympathy for my steward outweighed my annoyance!

When the time comes for the final assessment, make your decisions and then, time permitting, ask your steward to taste the wines and then place them in order of preference. It is advisable for the judge to leave the show bench whilst this is being done. If you watch him, he may not be able to concentrate on the wines. On your return, compare his result with yours and where there are differences, re-taste those wines with him and explain the reasons for your placings. This can be a very useful experience for the steward as it is only at this stage that you can explain the subtle differences between wines of near equal quality. After the tasting, complete any necessary paper work and ask your steward to take the forms to the appropriate person.

Impress on your steward the necessity of leaving your section of the show bench in a clean and orderly condition.

NOW A FEW GENERAL HINTS FOR THE
STEWARDS

Report to the Convenor of Judges in good time for the stewards briefing.

Do not use perfumed after-shave or hair oil on the morning of your stewardship.

Lady stewards should not wear perfume or perfumed make up.

Make sure that your hands are clean before judging commences.

Never smoke in the judging hall until all judging has been completed.

Make sure that the judge is kept supplied with drinking water.

Ensure that water for rinsing the glasses is at the show bench before the start of tasting.

Rinse the glasses after each tasting and either dry them, or stand them to drain as indicated by the judge.

If you wish to taste wines with the judge, ask if you can and provide two tasting glasses for your own use.

Do not offer comments about the wine until you are asked to do so.

Once judging has started, refrain from talking to the judge except to ask questions appertaining to judging procedure about which you are unsure.

Any other questions you may wish to ask, should be left until judging is finished.

Carry out such other duties as the judge may ask of you.

Remember at all times, that any remark the judge may make about the exhibits, is intended for your ears alone—they should under no circumstances be repeated to other persons, either inside or outside the judging hall.

If you are stewarding for the first time, tell your judge and make sure that you understand what is required of you before judging commences.

On completion of judging, make sure that you leave the bench in a clean and orderly condition.

Chapter 12
Judging Beers
by W. Newsom

In many ways the taste of the beer judge demands the same type of experience as that of the wine judge; one certainly cannot undertake it successfully without having undergone the necessary training. This means acquiring a good palate to detect the many nuances—both good and bad—which prevail in all beers, and having a thorough knowledge of practical brewing. Without this it is impossible to arrive at a verdict which involves understanding the use of the many types of grain, hops, mash temperatures, maturation and so on.

How does one set about getting this technical knowledge and practical experience? Take the latter first. The student, for that is what you are, should have the Guild of Judges Handbook and learn the section dealing with the judging of beers.

First, we must get together the necessary equipment. We need at least three glasses, which should be the balloon type with stem, capable of holding about 10 fluid ounces. The stem is important, for when judging the glass should be held by the foot to offset any chance of the nose picking up any scent from the hand, such as that of soap. We want two or more clean, dry glasscloths which do not leave a fluff deposit on the glass, a candle and candle-stick (or a small hand torch) to determine the clarity of the beer, and last, that very important tool, a crown cork opener. To keep our palate clean a non-fat biscuit such as Ryvita can be used. Water is the ideal palate cleanser but make sure that you bring it with you. This way you know the water quality. There is nothing worse than trying to judge beer where the local water is loaded with chlorine, or fluoride, or both! At no time should cheese or other fatty subjects be used as palate cleansers. The grease transfers itself from the mouth to the glass, causing the head and head retention to disappear. For the same reason when washing your glasses do not use a detergent. Plain warm water is all we need to use.

Having got together the equipment, we must have a yardstick by which to judge and the following system has really stood the test of time, so should be adopted. Each bottle should be judged under five headings, each being given the undivided attention of the judge. The five sections add up to a total of 30 points. The points to be awarded will be as follows:

Bottling, 2; Condition, 2; Clarity, 2; Bouquet, 4; Taste, Flavour, etc., 20; Total, 30.

We will go through each section, noting the ideal, and how the non-ideal are penalised.

BOTTLING

Here we examine the bottle. Should it be chipped, cracked, or scored it should be removed carefully from the rest of the bottles and disqualified on a point of safety. The bottle should be clean and polished, with a new crown cork or screw stopper with a rubber ring free from cracks or dirt. The bottle should be filled to within $\frac{1}{2}$ to $\frac{3}{4}$ inches of the closure. Full bottles should be eliminated on a point of safety. Those having greater air space than laid down should be penalised as this large air space can set up oxidisation, thus setting up beer spoilage. The yeast deposit in the bottle should be light and firm. Having taken all these factors into account, points will be deducted accordingly. There is nothing against awarding half points if it is thought that this will give a finer adjudication.

CONDITION

The beer should be judged in groups of three or more, keeping each bottle with its glass at all times until the judging is completed and the marks allocated. The head retention of all bitters, brown ales, and stouts should be full, with a fast moving bead. Lagers should have a higher CO_2 content thus giving a heavier head and faster bead. Barley Wine on the other hand should not retain a head but have a fast working bead. If there is head retention with a Barley Wine it is usually indicative that the alcoholic content is lower than one associates with this beer.

CLARITY

Beers should be star bright, that is to say brilliant to the eye, to gain the full points allocated. If a beer is just bright a deduction should be made. Opaque and heavily clouded beers should be penalised even further.

BOUQUET

Here the aroma or smell should be studied according to the type of beer under examination. Light ales should have a lightly hopped bouquet or 'nose'. **Pale ale** should have a more pronounced hopped bouquet. India Pale Ale or **Best Bitter** should have a nose of grain and hops—well balanced. **Brown ales** have a slightly "fruity" nose, and **Barley wines** be rich and fruity, reminiscent of a Christmas cake when it comes out of the oven!

TASTE

Here the judge should give his undivided attention to the many things that make up the looked-for character in the particular beer under surveillance. A light ale should be light in alcohol, refreshing and smooth to the palate. Pale ale is heavier in alcoholic content. The taste should prove to have a good balance in grain and hop. India pale ale or best bitter is the beer with the highest alcoholic content in this group of beers. There should be a pronounced taste of malt and hops. In all these beers there should be a pleasant dryness which should leave the palate clean and fresh after ejecting.

Brown ales vary considerably according to the locality where they are made. The judge should use his wide experience in assessing this class. A north east England brown ale can be fairly high in alcohol, amber in colour, with a residual sweetness. Some London brown ales, on the other hand, are extremely sweet, low in alcohol, and a deep brown in colour. A word of warning here. Do not judge any beer solely on colour. Remember the competitor may be trying to produce a product based on a local brew. To sum up this class, therefore, the judge should have a profound knowledge of this type of beer as produced throughout the country, but he should be aware that they should all be light in alcohol, with varying degrees of sweetness and colour. This will obviously give rise to taste differences.

Sweet stout is a light bodied beer with around $3\frac{1}{2}$ per cent alcohol. As soft water (as opposed to liquor used for bitters) is used the taste should be smooth. A pleasant hop and malt balance should be sought, and at all times the acidity should be low. The fully rounded flavour is the hall-mark of this beer. Two pitfalls to look for . . . the over-use of black malt or caramel. The experienced judge will detect this when taking the bouquet; the beginner should follow his example.

Dry stout is a great charactered beer, robust and pleasant. The alcoholic strength is about five per cent, with a deep liquorice colour and a head of deep oatmeal. The taste should be fully grained and very dry. A further character is the full body in the taste, with a slightly bitter and 'iron like' aftertaste. As this is derived from the use of black and chocolate malts the judge should again look for the over use of these which will give off-balance.

Lager is a difficult beer for an amateur to produce so the judge must bring all his experience to bear when judging this class. Be warned, many of the beers one judges will be light ales with seedless hops! Therefore it is imperative that one is au fait with both the production and taste of both commercial and amateur lagers. Most of the continental lagers have a starting gravity of about 1060°, whilst British lagers range around 1040°–1045°. This must also be taken into account. The taste should be round, fresh and very clean on the palate. A full flavour derived from the lager malt and seedless hops. This will ideally give the lager a crisp dryness. The head and bead should be faster and more retained than in bitter beer due to the higher CO_2 content.

Barley wine is a beer or blend of beers of wine-like quality. As the starting gravity can range from 80°–100° the alcoholic content will be very high. In like manner the residual sweetness will vary considerably from about 5°–19°. If the beer has been made correctly there will be little or no head retention, but a fast working bead will be noted (similar to champagne). This is due to the high alcohol. If there is a head retention one can suspect that the alcohol is less than required. The taste should be smooth, round and 'fruity'. As barley wine has this high degree of alcohol it has to be stored for anything up to two years to reach maturity. This should be duly noted.

Having dissected these beer types the judge should be aware of the many imperfections which can beset a beer. All beers can get autolysis. This is the break down of the yeast cells and confers an off-taste. Long maturing beers are most likely to be affected by autolysis. This should not be confused with a yeast-bitten beer, which has a harsh, bitter taste which can make the beer undrinkable. Roughness on the palate usually indicates an immature beer. A cheese-like bouquet and taste is attributed to a very poor or 'cheesy' hop. High acidity in any beer should be penalised. Diseased beers must obviously receive special attention.

Rope—This disease is recognised as strands of

bacteria joined together like rope suspended in the beer. If recognised in bottle do not open, mark bottle 'diseased beer' and remove from the show bench. If the bottle has been opened before recognition take the same action with the bottle, but thoroughly wash glass several times in very hot water. This disease is contagious to other beers, hence this action.

Slime forming yeasts—There are many forms of this type of disease. One type is named *rhodotorula mucilaginosa* and is instantly recognised as it turns the beer into a thick, oil-like substance. If the bottle is opened and poured into a glass it will have varying ranges of viscosity dependent on the amount of infection. The same strict procedure should be employed as for rope.

Pastorianus I, II, III—These are wild yeast forming turbidity in beer. Here the beer will be opaque, even cloudy, and will pour with a heavy head. It will be up to the judge to decide whether the competitors entry should be disqualified.

Draught beers will be judged in bouquet and taste as for bottled beers, but it must be remembered that draught beer takes on a different character from its bottled counterpart, being softer to the taste and with less CO_2 content. The beer referred to is of course a naturally carbonated beer which uses a priming sugar or syrup to create gas pressure in the barrel. When drawn off the beer should be star-bright. Cloudiness will be caused through inefficient fining or a flocculent yeast. Should a small portion of hop get through the tap make some allowance, for the beer may have been dry hopped. Whilst draught beers can be infected with the same diseases as bottled beers one further fault can manifest itself.

This is oxidisation. A beer can have been in a barrel which is only slowly being emptied. The ever growing air space and time will infect the beer with oxidisation.

One should at all times take note of the weather conditions prevailing at the time of judging for this has a profound effect on any beer under review. If the weather is hot or very hot care must be taken in opening the bottle for the compressed gas will be high in these conditions, causing the beer to be 'fussy'. A large head retention and fast working bead plus the warmth means that the judge has to exercise patience until the beer loses some of its head. Failure to do this will mean that the judge will not be taking the true bouquet but will be smelling concentrated CO_2 which is not very pleasant. In hot weather the warm beer will be cloying on the palate. If a beer has been over primed it will cascade out of the bottle in the form of froth and it is doubtful if the judge will have anything left to judge!

In cold weather different conditions will prevail. Beer left in draughts or cold conditions will become 'starved', that is to say dull and uninteresting. Listen carefully as the bottle is opened for the small hiss of gas as it escapes to atmosphere. If this is absent it means that the beer is flat and not starved. On pouring the head retention will be poor and the bead sluggish. The taste will be dull. It must be noted here that if the beers have been made correctly ALL the beers will be equally affected by these conditions. Should a beer hold a full head under these conditions it can be reasonably assumed that it has been over primed.

It should be remembered that the correct temperature for serving bitters should be 58°F., stouts and brown ales 60°–61°F., barley wines around 63°F., (to bring out the bouquet), whilst lagers should be served at about 56°F., to preserve the crispness and fast bead. You, being the judge, will never get these Utopian conditions, but there is no reason why you should not acquaint show organisers with this information. Who knows, at your next invitation some enterprising organiser might have done something about it!

When you have been allocated your steward to assist you in your task ask if he is interested in judging beers. If the answer is in the affirmative take him under your wing, and if the time is available (and this is important) go through the entries giving him the benefit of your knowledge, being very careful that he knows he must treat anything you impart as strictly confidential. Should you have a large class to judge you may have to forgo this help. Remember: the adjudication should at all times come first.

Never leave your judging sheet for all to see. This is a very personal document and may be misinterpreted if seen by others. At most shows it is usual for the judge to remain by the class he or she has judged to help competitors with any questions they may have regarding their entries. Tact is of the utmost importance, Try to be constructive, and not destructive in your remarks. Help competitors to rectify their faults by giving them the benefit of your experience. Your competitor will soon identify himself as a skilled brewer or a complete novice, so usually the former will not need your knowledge, whilst the latter will be only too pleased to seek it. There are times when a novice, due to a lack of

AMATEUR WINEMAKERS' NATIONAL GUILD OF JUDGES

VENUE _Middlesex Festival_ DATE _16th October_

JUDGE _WILF. NEWSOM_ CLASS _BARLEY WINE_

MARKING SHEET

EXB. No.	Presentation	Clarity	Bouquet	Flavour Balance Quality General Impression	Total	EXB. No.	REMARKS
3	2	2	1	11	16	3	POOR CONDITION. Faint bqt. Poor quality
4	1	3	2	13	19	4	CONDITION GOOD. BUT GD. TASTE LACKS STRENGTH
6						6	N.A.S.
7	2	3	3	16	24+	7	Excellent. Matured. Correct strength.
8	2	1	1	10	14	8	NO QUALITY ANYWHERE. FLAT. INSIPID
11	1	2	2	12	17	11	DIRTY BOTTLE, BOT. FAIR. THIN IN TASTE
12	2	3	2	15	22+	12	GOOD QUALITY. MORE HOPS WOULD IMPROVE TASTE
13	1	1	1	10	13	13	HIGH ACID. NO CONDITION, BAD QUALITY. DIRTY BOTTLE
14	2	2	2	14	20	14	TOO much head. Taste & bouquet fair. WEAK.
15	1	NIL	1	9	11	15	FLAT. NO CONDITION, TASTE OR BOUQUET.
21	2	4	3	16	25	21	SUPERB BEER. WELL CONDITIONED. WELL BALANCED
22						22	Diseased beer. See competitor.

RESULT: 1ST. 21

2ND. 7 } ONLY THREE AWARDS MADE

3RD. 12

knowledge, has difficulty in answering salient questions or asking questions regarding his or her problems. In such cases the judge should be Sherlock Holmes, Peter Wimsey, and Father Brown rolled into one. By a slow process of deduction one can invariably find the answer to the problem. Why go to all this trouble? The answer is twofold. First, the problem represents a challenge, and a good judge should welcome a challenge. Second, the judge should with some humility remember that he or she never ceases to learn. There is not, nor ever will be, a place for a judge who thinks he knows it all.

Chapter 13
The Guild of Judges

The revival of the art of making wine in the home started in the mid 1950's and gathered momentum with the end of sugar rationing in 1953. The speed with which the movement grew must be one of the most significant achievements of any hobby in this or any other country.

This rapid growth brought in its wake a number of problems; one of these was the problem of judging the wine exhibits at the many shows, the number of which grew rapidly towards the end of the decade. The number of winemaking societies increased and they in turn held their own local wine competitions. Some of the societies amalgamated to form larger shows and the first such Amateur Winemakers Festival was held at Hertford in the year 1959.

With the improvement of organisation, growth continued, culminating in the first National Show which was held at Andover in 1959 and comprised six classes. Of course, many anomalies existed between the judges, drawn from local societies by recommendation. These judges were the more experienced winemakers who had established themselves locally as having a good palate and the ability to judge wine. However, the procedure adopted for judging gave a certain amount of concern amongst the exhibitors who, in many cases, were of the opinion that one won a prize more by luck than by judgement. Some Horticultural Shows were beginning to include wine classes in their schedules, and the position was further complicated by the employment at these of persons to judge wine classes who were not even winemakers. Two examples will adequately describe the situation:

At one such show, an exhibitor collecting his exhibits, found the level of wine in his bottles apparently untouched and this applied to all the other exhibits. He asked the Show Official when the wines were being judged and was informed that the wines had already been judged.

"But", remarked the exhibitor, "how could they have been? The level of wine is still the same!"

"Oh well" replied the Official, "the lady just dipped her little finger into the neck of the bottle and then sucked it!"

On the second occasion, the lady had a much better technique. She poured wine into a teaspoon and then tasted it!

In these days of more sophisticated wine tasting, these two examples sound like tall stories. These were, of course, extreme cases but quite obviously something had to be done, and without delay, if the hobby was to gain credence. Remember, in those days we were fighting very hard to lift the level of our hobby from that of a music hall joke to one worth serious consideration, and even dedication.

In 1963, the matter was fully discussed by the Committee of the Amateur Winemakers National Conference. The Committee members realised the situation was fraught with difficulties but were in general agreement that something had to be done. As a preliminary step, I, as Convenor of Judges for the 1964 National Show, was asked to prepare a standard procedure to be adopted by the judges selected for that show.

In the meantime, a sub-committee was formed to discuss the problems and the possibility of forming a National Guild of Judges. The sub-committee met in the summer of 1963 and after many hours of deliberation and discussion, it was decided to recommend to the National Conference Committee that the judges selected for the 1964 Conference be invited to form a Guild of Judges under the aegis of the National Conference Committee.

The Conference judges met in November 1963 and unanimously agreed to standardise methods and procedure of judging and form an association to be known as The Amateur Winemakers National Guild of Judges. A committee was formed to prepare a handbook which would contain a standard procedure for judges, along with other relevant material appertaining to show organisation, and which would become the text book for the examination for future candidates for The Guild. This was done, and the handbook approved and adopted by a general meeting of The Guild in the early summer of 1964.

The thoroughness and careful thought to detail given by the Handbook Committee is borne out by the fact that although that little handbook has had three revisions, all have been of a minor nature. The present edition includes a procedure for the judging of beer, prepared by a committee of beer judges from The Guild. Many members of The Guild are qualified, by examination, to judge both wine and beer.

The Guild was originally formed by 47 Founder Members; 212 members have passed through the register to 1975 and the present membership is 195. Entry to the Guild can only be gained by passing an examination, a prospectus for which can be obtained from the Hon. Sec. of the Guild. The standard required to pass the examination is a high one, but although the pass rate is fairly low, the fact remains that between 160 and 170 candidates have met the required standards since the commencement of the examination. Those who fail at the first attempt can retake the examination after a year, as indeed many have done—successfully. The unsuccessful candidates are informed where their weakness lies and are then able to concentrate on remedying that particular aspect. As the examination is in three parts, and provided the unsuccessful candidate applies to retake the examination within two years, any part which he has passed does not have to be retaken.

The Guild organises examinations annually in various parts of the country, from Leeds in the north to Torquay in the west, and is prepared to send a panel of adjudicators to any part of the country where a demand exists. This, of course, is an expensive exercise in these days of high travelling costs, so that a minimum number of candidates is required in any given area before such an examination can be set up. A suitable venue has to be found which will meet the requirements of the examination, and to hire such premises for a full day can be quite costly.

The A.W.N.G.J. has, over the years, assumed

international standing. One member flew over from America to obtain the necessary qualification for the examination, and came over the following year to take the examination. He wanted to be the first American to pass the Guild Examination. The Guild also has two members in Canada and one in Holland. The Rhodesian Guild of Judges, which is moulded on similar lines, is affiliated to the A.W.N.G.J. and one of its members has also taken the examination in this country.

Members of The Guild are kept very busy judging at shows all over the country, from circle level to the major wine shows. It is estimated from returns supplied by members of The Guild that during the year 1975, between them they judged 80,000 bottles of wine at 2,000 engagements—a truly remarkable record.

A National Wine Judge is expected, by the exhibitor, to give an authoritative answer to any question on the practice of winemaking and the after care of wine. He must, therefore, know his subject thoroughly. This is one of the reasons why that subject is part of the examination of the A.W.N.G.J. and, although the would-be judge is not expected to be a scientist or biologist, he is expected to know a little elementary science, have some knowledge of enzymes and their functions and also know varieties of yeasts, their action, and reproduction insofar as they concern winemaking.

Before taking the examination, the candidate should have a good basic knowledge of hygiene in winemaking practice and equipment, of selecting the best ingredients for producing the different types of wine, the preparation of the must and various methods of sterilising it and must be prepared to discuss the relative merits of each method. He must also be able to balance the must prior to fermentation, know acids and their use in winemaking, the relevant strengths in the various types of wine, and express this acidity as parts per thousand or percentage. A basic knowledge of acid titration would be an advantage.

The candidate must know about sugars, both fermentable and non-fermentable, and the sugar/alcohol ratio. He must be able to consider the various factors when adjusting the must, know how to use a hydrometer, the meaning of specific gravity, and sugar/gravity relationship. He must be conversant with tannin and its use in wine, with yeast, yeast reproduction, their effects on wine and how they are affected by high sugar or alcohol content. Also about yeast growth during fermentation, how it is affected by temperature, and about aerobic and anaerobic fermentations. He should know about pulp fermentation and its effect on wine. He must know when to use yeast nutrient, also about enzymes and their application in winemaking. The candidate must know which essentials of wine are derived from the basic ingredients and which from fermentation. He must be able to give the reasons for racking wine, clarification, hazes, their origin, recognition and correction, stabilisation and general after care of wine, know about storage containers and their relative merits. He must recognise disorders in wine caused by contamination, bacteria and other spoilage organisms. The candidate will also be asked questions on the contents of The Handbook of the A.W.N.G.J., (obtainable from A.W. Publications Ltd., South Street, Andover).

In addition to the two oral sections, the candidate will have a practical test in wine evaluation. This is fully described in the examination prospectus, obtainable on application to the Hon. Secretary of The Guild. The examination, as you can see, is a thorough one, but is by no means terrifying to any reasonably experienced winemaker with a good palate.

To obtain a pass and be admitted to The Guild is an honour which amply repays the hard work involved in studying for the examination. At the same time, it is but the beginning of the continual process of learning the art of judging wine.

BIBLIOGRAPHY

DAVISON, H. (1962). *Physiology of the Eye*. 2nd. Ed. London.

ADEY, E.R. (1959). *The Sense of Smell in Handbook of Physiology Sec*. 1. Vol. 1 Washington D.C.

GREEN, J. H. (1963). *An introduction to Human Physiology*. Oxford University Press, London.

SYLVESTER, P. E. (1964). *Applied Anatomy and Physiology for Nurses*. Blackwell Scientific Publications, Oxford.

AMERINE, M. A., ROESSLER E. B. and FILIPELLO F. *Modern Sensory Methods of Evaluating Wine. Hilgardia*. Vol. 28. (1959). University of California.

FISCHER, R. and GRIFFIN, F. (1961). *Experientia*.

SAMSON WRIGHTS *Applied Physiology* 4th Ed. (1965). Oxford University Press.

Dr. JURGEN SCHEIDE. *Physiology of the Sense of Smell and Taste*.

INDEX